O and M for First-Line Managers

O and M for First-Line Managers

Stanley Oliver
C.Eng., M.I.Mech.E., M.I.Prod.E., A.M.B.I.M., F.R.S.A.
Senior Lecturer in Management Techniques, Salford College of Technology

Edward Arnold

© S. Oliver 1975

First published in 1975 by
Edward Arnold (Publishers) Ltd.
25 Hill Street, London W1X 8LL

ISBN: 0 7131 3350 3

All Rights Reserved. No part of this publication may be reproduced, stored in a retrieval system, or transmitted in any form or by any means, electronic, mechanical, photocopying, recording or otherwise, without the prior permission of Edward Arnold (Publishers) Ltd.

Printed in Great Britain by
The Camelot Press Ltd, Southampton

Preface

The expression 'first-line manager' is meant to include management personnel carrying such titles as foreman, superintendent and supervisor, although, for reasons of convenience, the expression 'supervisor' is used throughout the text.

To give a brief idea of the book's scope, Chapter 1 is a consideration of the financial background to O and M work and the need for control: the supervisor's place is explained and emphasized. This is linked in Chapter 2 with the place of O and M in the supervisor's organization; the thorny question of O and M's consultative nature is also explained. Chapter 3 explains important organizational principles and Chapters 4, 5, 6 and 7 deal with the work study basis of O and M, covering the building of a standard time and its subsequent integration with the work specification and incentive schemes, and the important techniques of activity sampling and method study. Chapter 8 deals with clerical work measurement and Chapter 9 attempts to familiarize the supervisor with the area of specialist techniques, such as operational research and systems analysis. Chapter 10 deals with general aspects, such as report writing, office machines and systems, and the final chapter is a discussion of the vital human aspect of O and M work.

This book is written primarily for supervisors, both in office and workshop situations, and will also be of interest to students taking examinations for professional courses. Office supervisors are clearly in the front line of O and M activities, but workshop supervisors are very much at the receiving end of paperwork systems and administrative decisions. The O and M practitioner is not just another specialist: the results of his work may be radical changes to the supervisor's environment and the systems within which he operates. The effects of searching O and M investigations demand the attention of the progressive supervisor.

S. O.

Acknowledgements

I would like to express my appreciation to the following organizations for giving permission to quote typical or past examinations questions: The Institute of Work Study Practitioners, 9/10 River Front, Enfield, Middlesex; The National Examination Board in Supervisory Studies, 76 Portland Place, London W1N 4AA; The City and Guilds of London Institute, 76 Portland Place, London W1; The Institution of Works Managers, 45 Cardiff Road, Luton, Bedfordshire LU1 1RQ.

I am also deeply indebted to the British Standards Institution for granting permission to use many of their definitions in BS 3138:1969 'Glossary of Terms Used in Work Study'. Copies of the complete standards may be obtained from the Institution at BS House, 2 Park Street, London W1A 2BS.

A management book of this type inevitably draws on personal experience and I wish to thank the following organizations where I was allowed to practise management before entering the teaching profession: Thorn Industries Ltd.; Rolls-Royce Ltd. (Aero Engine Division); City of Manchester; County Borough of Rochdale; The Oilwell Engineering Co. Ltd.; Hawker Siddeley Ltd.; Crossley Motors Ltd.

Finally, I wish to thank my wife Christine for typing the manuscript, for valuable editorial work and for her general encouragement and patience in accepting the inevitable interference with domestic routine. Also, my thanks to my wife's parents, for the use of their seaside chalet, where much of the groundwork for this book was done.

Contents

Preface   v

Acknowledgements   vi

Chapter 1 **The nature and aims of O and M**   1
Control; standards and performance; financial background; O and M work study; O and M personnel; the management services concept; the supervisor's contribution; examination questions

Chapter 2 **The working basis of O and M**   14
The general place of O and M; relationships with other departments; relationships with trades unions; relationships with supervisors; management directives and the consultative role; examination questions

Chapter 3 **The study of organization**   24
Purpose; organizational definitions; formal and informal organizational relationships; company organizational structure; principles of organization; company size; company type; centralization and decentralization; manuals and responsibility charts; examination questions

Chapter 4 **Applied work study principles—the standard time**   45
Work study procedure; critical examination; the standard time; examination questions

Chapter 5 **Statistical aids**   59
Methods and examples: descriptive statistics; inductive statistics; standard deviation; averages; skewed distribution; number of readings; correlation coefficients; activity sampling; examination questions

Chapter 6 **Applied work study principles—uses of work measurement, specification, payment, planning and cost controls** 82
The uses of work measurement; work specification; payment; planning and cost controls; examination questions

Chapter 7 **Applied work study principles—method study charting** 99
Process sequence charts; movement charts; time-scale charts; miscellaneous charts; examination questions

Chapter 8 **Clerical work measurement** 117
Definitions; the need; special problems; time study; systems; examination questions

Chapter 9 **Specialist O and M techniques** 129
Systems analysis; operational research; examination questions

Chapter 10 **General aspects of O and M** 144
Report writing; form design; office machines; mechanical aids in communication; office systems; examination questions

Chapter 11 **Human aspects** 159
The nature of O and M; resistance to change; meeting ground; conflict; Taylor's 'Scientific Management'; attitudes; O and M negotiation; examination questions

Index 175

1
The nature and aims of O and M

> Organization and methods is 'a management service, the object of which is to increase the administrative efficiency of an organization by improving procedures, methods and systems, communications and controls, and organization structure.'
>
> (British Standard BS 3138: 1969)

1.1 Control

Supervisors studying management subjects will notice that some words are repeatedly used in the management vocabulary; one of these words is control. This is convenient, since control is a word normally used by supervisors in their everyday lives. It is used in practically every sport; football enthusiasts, for example, will talk of a controlled delivery of the ball, a footballer bringing the ball under control, and so on. In the management sense, they will talk of a football captain controlling the game, without necessarily analyzing how he is achieving the control. For example, do the supporters analyze his captaincy into several roles such as on the field of play, during training sessions, and his social contact with his players?

The concept of control is fairly simple to discuss because of its yes—no nature. A person either has control or does not have it: he is either gaining control or losing it. In the management of industrial, commercial, governmental, or other complex organizations, control is a fundamental requirement if success is to be achieved.

The primary function of business management is to protect the owners' interests by directing the company or organization towards sound objectives which will ensure future profitable, effective and efficient existence. Hence the main purpose of control is the setting of financial and other standards for all business activity in order to achieve an acceptable, planned profit or performance, and the measurement of performance against pre-set standards.

It should be appreciated by supervisors at this stage that business organizations vary tremendously according to the type of work undertaken. Organization and methods (O and M) officers are employed in such diverse organizations as industry, insurance, hospitals, local government and central government. The paragraphs above have accordingly been written with care, bearing this in mind.

The elements of success for a commercial business may be stated as follows:
1. Making a marketable product
2. Maintaining an acceptable quality standard
3. Manufacturing to achieve an acceptable price
4. Ensuring sales

However, if we compare these elements with the objectives of local government, for example, important modifications need to be made. The one great difference between local government and industry is that the main objective of local government is to provide a service to the community. Hence the elements of success for local government can be listed as:
1. Supplying the service required
2. Maintaining an acceptable quality standard
3. Achieving these objectives at the least cost to the rates

In local government or hospital O and M work, the elements of success must be observed in this order, with 'service required' as a definite first. We can illustrate this by a simple example. Costs could be reduced in a local authority by cutting the staffing of health inspectors by one-half. The result would be a loss of control in areas such as meat inspection and general catering establishments. An epidemic could result, with serious illness or avoidable deaths in the community. It would be no surprise to find members of the O and M department losing face or even their positions in such circumstances, and rightly so if it was their suggestion.

It can be seen from this small example that it is futile to view local government or hospitals in the same light as factories producing bicycles, iron castings or packets of soap. The object of these organizations is to provide a service and they should be administered as such.

1.2 Standards and performance

The supervisor will also notice that the word standard occurs frequently in management vocabulary. A standard is simply a point of reference, provided as a guide to the various people involved, and relating to a range of activities or aspects. For example, some standard groups are headed: quality; labour; material; service; safety; goodhousekeeping; industrial relations; procedural. We have already stated that the main purpose of control includes the setting of financial and other standards. It is now opportune to state that one of the prime functions of work study is the setting of accurate standards in as many areas of the business as possible.

The list of standards we have already mentioned is fairly self-explanatory, but an expansion of one of the aspects may be helpful. When

The nature and aims of O and M

we talk of labour standards, we are referring to the time that a piece of work should take to complete. That is a simple statement, with an apparently simple objective. However, in practice it can become a very difficult objective to achieve and much trouble has been caused in industry by unqualified people attempting to set accurate and fair standards. The question of how long a job should take raises a number of difficult questions, such as:
1. What is the best method to use?
2. What type of worker is required (or available) to do it?
3. What should be the precise nature of the available or achievable environment?
4. What training should be given, or has been given, to the worker?
5. What incentive should be given to the worker?

No matter how difficult it may be to set standards, the effort will always be worthwhile and the supervisor can be a tremendous help to the work study officer.

The main reasons for using standards are:
1. To ensure the most efficient use of labour and materials
2. To enable management to plan the future work programme accurately
3. To enable management to balance the work load across the organization
4. To provide a sound basis for estimating and price-fixing

Performance is the out-working of standards. The keys to management control are the continual striving to achieve standards and the necessary revision of standards in the light of experience. Performance is another of our common management words and most supervisors will probably have experienced performance-criticism from their managers.

Many supervisors complain, understandably, of not really knowing their objectives. Such supervisors inevitably work in organizations where accurate and comprehensive standards are non-existent: their complaints that they do not know how well they are performing pass unheeded. It is in such companies that a newly-appointed O and M officer can be very helpful to both management and supervisors.

1.3 Financial background

In the early days of O and M, its object was to produce substantial, directly measurable cost savings, providing a known-ratio return on the O and M overhead expenditure. In recent years, it has become increasingly obvious that some of the key areas of management activity needing O and M analysis and recommendations are those where increased effectiveness is not directly measurable in terms of money. Nevertheless, most O and M work will reduce costs, whether they are directly measurable or not.

The aims of O and M generally are to achieve one or more of the following objectives:
1. Direct (measurable) cost savings
2. Increased efficiency and effectiveness
3. Improved working conditions

Point 2 includes those projects which clearly improve the efficiency of a service to management, but which may be difficult to measure in terms of money saved. Increased efficiency may be very clearly evident, however, in the reduction of time delays between procedures. In one very large manufacturing company, for example, the time needed to make production castings from a new component design was nine months, due to the complex nature of the work. Great efforts were made to reduce this lead time and a one-week achievement would have been considered remarkably good. It was not possible, however, to measure the financial implications. After a certain amount of lead-time reduction one could reach a position where a company was beating its competitors on the market and enormous orders could be won.

Point 3 includes those projects which clearly improve the working environment in such a way as to create a more contented work force. This may be done, for example, by introducing better workplace layouts, equipment and general facilities. Direct cost savings might result from the subsequent reduced labour turnover and increased productivity, but the benefits are not always easy to measure in direct terms.

Effectiveness and efficiency. Although one situation is showing a higher productivity than another, it is not necessarily more effective than the other. For example, important factors may include consideration of whether excessive rates of payment have been made for the work and whether the sales force is effective in selling and distributing the product.

Consider the example of a man painting an article in two hours, using an efficient method: consider also the alternative of ten men painting the same article in one hour. This could be a more effective performance, but we should remember that efficiency is concerned with doing a job with the least waste and cost. In the first case the time content is two hours and may be taken to be a measure of productivity (that is, half an article per hour per man). In the second case the time content is ten hours, which is five times as much time. The new productivity is one-tenth of an article per hour per man, which is only one-fifth of the earlier manpower productivity. The first situation shows a much better productivity than the second. However, as far as production is concerned, the production over a two hour period in the first case would be one article, and in the second case it would be two articles (that is, double the amount of production). This could be considered more effective in some circumstances.

If the rate of pay for a painter is 50p per hour, then the labour costs per article, respectively, would be 100p and 500p. However, if we are painting two articles against a customer's deadline, with the real chance of securing

The nature and aims of O and M

a further order of 10 000 articles, the second method is the most effective in this situation, although more costly at the time.

Individual sections of a shipyard could have high productivity, and could be described as operating efficiently as platelayers, fitters and so on, but if they do not work together effectively, orders may be lost due to poor delivery dates.

'Getting the job done properly' implies the whole range of good management which requires the achievement of all objectives with the minimum use of resources. For further discussion of this area see 'How the Japanese Mind Works' by Edward de Bono (*Financial Times*, 5th October, 1971) and 'Japanese Effectiveness and Efficiency' (*Financial Times*, 12th October, 1971) by Stanley Oliver.

O and M in financial control. As mentioned earlier, we are concerned with safeguarding the future profitable or effective existence of an organization. In working to these ends, it is not only the owners' interests that are served, but also those of the employees in providing relatively assured employment.

A financial plan is generally best looked at from the viewpoint of profitability. Figure 1.1 shows this in diagrammatic form for a manufacturing company, through a marginal-costing break-even chart. Supervisors are no doubt conversant with the break-even chart, particularly present or past students of NEBSS, IWSP and IWM.

Briefly, the object of the chart is to plot the sales income of the company

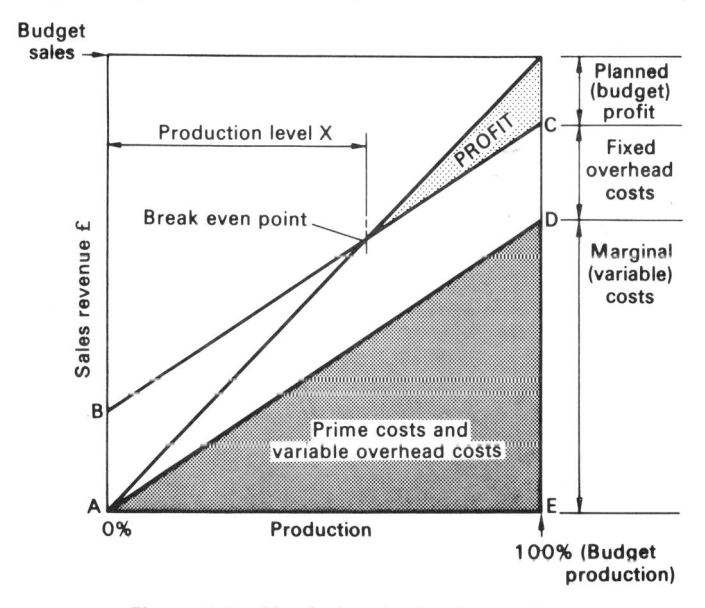

Figure 1.1 Marginal costing break-even chart

against a base of production achievement. For example, referring to Figure 1.1, the budget production could represent 200 000 raincoats for a clothing factory and the budget sales could represent their sales value, say £2 million. In this type of break-even chart, the fixed overhead costs represented by area ABCD, are superimposed on to the variable cost line AD. After the break-even point has been reached, at the production level X, the profit increases until the planned year-end profit is achieved. A profit is only made if the sales revenue exceeds the sum of the fixed overhead costs and the marginal (variable) costs. The latter costs comprise variable overhead costs and the prime costs of production (direct labour, direct material and direct expenses) as shown in Figure 1.2.

The financial plan, then, is to hold the planned profit in the face of continually increasing costs and often in a competitive market. Market competition will restrict price increases but the marginal (variable) costs will tend to rise above expected levels due to many factors such as materials price increases, pay awards, increases in power charges and so on.

In the case of the fixed overhead costs it is interesting to note the meaning of 'fixed'. Costs are so designated if, in the reasonably short term, they are constant over an agreed output range (for example, plus or minus 10 per cent). In practice, a company should be able to set up a fairly predictable financial framework for a period of one year ahead, but it is still possible to receive some nasty shocks in this area within such a short period. Unexpected staff pay awards, basic power cost increases, insurance, rent and rates increases, advertising costs to meet unexpected competition and increases in sundry costs such as telephone and stationery are just some of the cost increases which may need to be combated if an attractive profit margin is to be maintained.

Standard costing. This is a system of comparing actual events in a manufacturing process with estimated or predetermined standards of cost and performance. Divergencies (known as variances) from standards are promptly reported, with the aim of allowing true causes to be diagnosed and the necessary corrective action to be taken immediately. It is the function of cost accounting.

The overall process of managing a business by observing and acting upon divergencies (or variances) from pre-set standards is known as management by exception: this is an extremely important principle of management.

Budgetary control. This relates expenditure to the person incurring the expenditure; it normally takes the form of departmental budgets or allocated amounts of expenditure to be regularly monitored. The aims are to plan the business policy, co-ordinate business activities and control individual business functions.

There are a large number of possible budgets in a sizeable manufacturing company but a supervisor will fit into a sub-section of one.

Marginal (variable) costs

Costs which tend to vary directly or proportionately with the number of articles or units produced.

A. *Prime costs*
1. Direct cost of raw materials and bought-out components used in the manufacture of products.
2. Direct labour: earnings of operatives engaged in the manufacture and, where applicable, the inspection of products.
3. Direct expenses: tooling, pattern and draughting costs which are incurred specifically for known jobs, providing that they are either totally consumed or may be legitimately written off after use.

In direct expenses we may also include overtime premium payments for known and readily identified jobs where such overtime was expected, and overtime premium payments, as a result of special additional requests by customers and where they are paying for the additional unexpected work. Also included in direct expenses may be any special work providing it is only applicable to a specific job; for example, special tests and experiments.

B. *Variable overhead costs*
These costs may be considered to vary proportionately to output. Examples:
Electrical power (excluding any maximum demand charges)
Cost of raising steam which is used for the manufacturing process
Auxiliary materials used in the production process; for example, lubricants, solvents, cutting fluids, abrasives, powders, cleaning materials
Packing materials
Carriage and freight
Telephone costs: variable element
Commission earned by salesmen
Bonuses (if any) earned by production supervision
Scrap and rectification costs.
Other lost time costs
Premium (overtime) payments for general overtime to meet normal production commitments
Non- (directly) productive service labour costs: for example labourers engaged in feeding machines or otherwise closely working with direct personnel

Fixed overhead costs

Costs which must be recovered, but which, in a reasonably short term, are virtually unchanged over an agreed output range of, for example, plus or minus 10% on budget.
Each article or product should carry its fair share of these costs, which are often referred to as fixed overheads. Examples:
Electrical power maximum demand charges
Maintenance costs
Cost of raising steam which is used for general factory heating
Salaries of management and administration personnel
Salesmen's basic salaries
Basic salaries of production supervisors, foremen and 'non-working' charge-hands
Wages of machine setters, general labourers, apprentices and trainees
Inspection and storekeeping costs
Internal transport costs
Toolroom costs
Welfare, health and canteen costs
Office costs in administration areas
Office costs in manufacturing areas
Sales costs
Depreciation of plant and buildings
Maintenance of roadways and factory buildings
Insurances
Rents and rates charges
Security costs (e.g. factory police)
Advertising costs
Various subscriptions
Sundry costs such as stationery, postage: telephone costs, basic (fixed) charge, travelling expenses
Various fees: legal, consultancy, accountancy, etc.
Research, design and development costs
Holiday pay and National Insurance contributions for direct workers

Figure 1.2 Division of manufacturing costs

It is therefore necessary for each supervisor to understand his own budget and its part in the whole. Manufacturing supervisors, for example, should be involved in the budgets for production, labour and works expenses. It is vital that a very close control is kept on materials and labour costs. Accurate standard costs will require sound work study.

1.4 O and M and work study

O and M is defined as 'a management service, the object of which is to increase the administrative efficiency of an organization by improving procedures, methods and systems, communications and controls, and organization structure' (British Standard BS 3138: 1969). Supervisors should note particularly that O and M is a service to them and should not attempt to erode their position as line managers. It is also of direct interest since it deals mainly with organization and administrative problems and thus concerns itself with the supervisor's paperwork, communications and organization problems.

Work study has been simply defined as 'the study of work with the object of achieving economy'. However, since the nature of work has become very complicated, a more detailed definition is required, such as that given by the British Standards Institute (BS 3138: 1969): 'A management service based on those techniques, particularly method study and work measurement, which are used in the examination of human work in all its contexts, and which lead to the systematic investigation of all the resources and factors which affect the efficiency and economy of the situation being reviewed, in order to effect improvement.'

Once again supervisors should note that they are receiving a service. The overall aim is, very clearly, to obtain an improvement in efficiency and general effectiveness. Specific mention is made of method study and work measurement and these are important enough to merit some expansion (BS 3138: 1969): 'Method study is the systematic recording and critical examination of the factors and resources involved in existing and proposed ways of doing work, as a means of developing and applying easier and more effective methods and reducing costs. Work measurement is the application of techniques designed to establish the time for a qualified worker to carry out a specified job at a defined level of performance.' These aspects will be discussed in considerable detail, in a later chapter.

Relationship. There is sometimes unnecessary confusion as to the relationship between O and M and work study.

The analytical principles of work study were laid down by pioneers such as Frederick Taylor (1856–1915) and Frank B. Gilbreth (1868–1924) in the USA. It was the amalgamation of Gilbreth's Motion Study and Taylor's efforts in the field of work measurement that created a grouping

The nature and aims of O and M

of techniques known for many years as Time and Motion Study. Naturally, the passing of time produced many refinements, due to further advances in knowledge and experience, and the body of experience and techniques is now assembled under the heading of work study. The subject gained universal acceptance and application in manufacturing areas long before the Second World War, but the rigorous application of work study principles to administrative areas of business did not commence, certainly in the UK, until after the war.

The main difference, then, between work study and O and M is in the area of application. O and M is usually seen in the concept of management services, this title often being synonymous with O and M. Another difference is that organization study is peculiar to O and M, especially in the wider aspect of total-company or total-organization context. Also, because O and M is expected to look at the whole organizational effort, it has had to develop and use complex techniques such as operational research (OR) and computers, in an effort to control the wider areas of business operation.

1.5 O and M personnel

Specialized personnel. There are definite advantages to be gained from using specialists in this field, for the following reasons:
1. It is important for the O and M officer to be impartial.
2. It is important for him to be outside the problem area, looking in. Many people in busy working situations are unable to be objective about their circumstances.
3. The efficient use of O and M demands a high level of background knowledge, based upon experience of the specialized techniques and both O and M and general business experience.
4. One of the benefits from using O and M is that the practitioners are given plenty of time to look at problems, without the encumbrances of line duties.

The job of O and M specialist demands a number of particular qualities, which can be conveniently grouped under three headings:
1. Education. Ideally, the specialist should be a professional, such as a professional engineer or accountant: this implies an education to degree level plus post-degree studies. He should also have received a substantial amount of education and training in the specialized techniques of work study, operational research, computers, statistics and psychology. He could hardly achieve the required maturity before the age of thirty years.
2. Experience. Much will depend on the major areas of development planned for a particular organization and the nature of the work. Figure 1.3 gives a working experience analysis of an imaginary O and M team in a sizeable engineering company, assuming that there

are four team members (not counting trainees). Let us assume that the team comprises:

professional engineer	age 40
professional accountant	age 30
commercial specialist	age 28
scientist/mathematician	age 30

Figure 1.3 is self-explanatory and gives an idea of the importance attached to experience in O and M work.

Area	Percentage of total working experience of four-man O and M team
Commercial	12
Engineering	18
Manufacturing	8
Accountancy	16
Computers (including maths/stats)	24
General O and M	22
TOTAL	100

Figure 1.3 Working experience of an imaginary O and M team in a sizeable manufacturing company

3. Personality. It is fairly obvious that O and M specialists must have high technical qualifications for the work. Unfortunately, many people overlook the personal qualities required, which are equally important: these include
   resilience and tenacity
   a real interest in change
   above-average patience
   a lively and creative imagination
   'progressive' curiosity
   above-average ability in speech and writing
   above-average ability to get on with people

1.6 The management services concept

The need for central management services departments grew out of the needs of large organizations. Management services departments often group together a number of specialisms under one head, as can be seen in the example of Figure 1.4. The logic behind this concentration of special skills and creative brainpower is sound and one or two concluding points will suffice:
   1. The management services manager has a normal collateral organizational relationship with line managers and he is also a functional manager, existing only to give a service to other line managers.

The nature and aims of O and M

2. Systems analysis is used in the sense of putting an information system on to a computer.
3. O and M is used in the sense of general work in a wide range of O and M activities, such as office incentive schemes, general office machinery, training and development schemes and communications and organizational problems. It also gives assistance to the systems analyst by providing whatever back-up service may be required in terms of already-available information on a particular department's organization and methods.

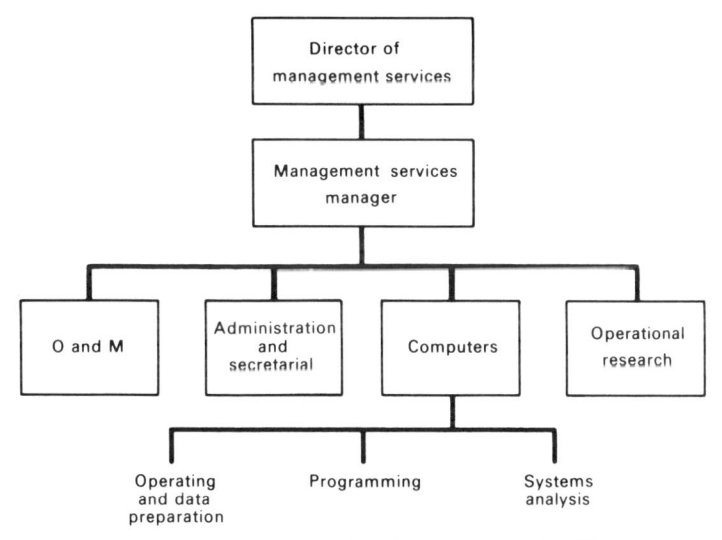

Figure 1.4 A management services department in a sizeable company

4. OR work is heavily dependent on masses of statistical information on company activities and it is logical to place OR workers in close association with O and M and systems analysis personnel.

The concept of a service, or functional department, will be discussed fully in the chapters dealing with the study of organization.

1.7 The supervisor's contribution

A supervisor, on reading what has gone before in this chapter, might be excused for thinking that the whole subject is so specialized that he could not possibly make a contribution. Nothing could be further from the truth.

One of the most important phases in an O and M investigation is the fact-gathering phase, and there are two points at which supervisors can make a contribution. Firstly, they can help at the general fact-finding stage, when the O and M practitioner requires paperwork, systems and statistical information from the supervisor. Secondly, there is need for assistance at the interviews-stage, when supervisors should take the opportunity to make suggestions for improvements in their departments' organization and methods.

No matter how new systems are devised, or who devises them, the person who has to work them is usually the supervisor. It is therefore vital for the supervisor to show interest in the implementation and succeeding stages of any new procedures.

Supervisors should establish a good relationship with their O and M departments. In this way they can help the company and themselves.

Examination questions

1. Why is it desirable to have a costing system in any business?
   (NEBSS Certificate, 1968)
2. Explain (i) fixed costs, (ii) variable costs.
   (NEBSS Certificate, 1969)
3. Give three examples of the use of costing.
   (NEBSS Certificate, 1969)
4. How frequently do you consider a supervisor who operates on an annual budget should be provided with progress information for effective control? Give reasons for your answer.
   (NEBSS Certificate, 1970)
5. Define work study and O and M. Expand the definition of work study and show how its techniques are applicable to O and M.
   (HND Business Studies)
6. (i) Draw up a list of the personal qualities looked for in the O and M officer.
   (ii) Why should it be necessary to have such a specialist?
   (iii) Draw up a programme for training O and M personnel.
   (HND Business Studies)
7. Define budgetary control and break-even point.
   (NEBSS Certificate, 1969)
8. Give three distinct examples of possible cost reduction in an organization with which you are familiar.
   (NEBSS Certificate, 1968)
9. Write an essay on work study, its definition, its main techniques and its relationship to other productivity services.
   (City & Guilds *Work Study*, 1969)
10. Define the term productivity. List ways in which productivity can be increased by work study.
    (City & Guilds *Work Study*, 1968)
11. Suggest the necessary steps to be taken to ensure the cost effectiveness

The nature and aims of O and M

of a works where 500 people are employed on the batch production of engineering components.

(IWM Specimen Examination Question, Works Management Theory and Practice)

12. Outline how you would establish a total standard cost for a product with which you are familiar.

(IWSP Graduate *Costing Aspects*, 1969)

13. (i) What are the overall objectives of organization and methods?
    (ii) Comment on the effectiveness of work measurement in the clerical field.

(IWSP *Associated Techniques A*, 1974)

14. (i) Construct a break-even chart from the following data for producing 50 000 units.

	Variable £	Fixed £	Total £
Direct labour	10 000		10 000
Direct material	20 000		20 000
Factory overheads	6 000	4 000	10 000
Selling	4 000	1 000	5 000
Administration		5 000	5 000
	40 000	10 000	50 000

(ii) What are the limitations of a break-even chart?

(IWSP *Costing Aspects*, 1974)

15. How can work study contribute to the effective control of costs?

(IWSP *Costing Aspects*, 1974)

16. (i) What is budgetary control?
    (ii) How does budgetary control differ from standard costing?

(IWSP *Costing Aspects*, 1973)

17. Explain how a cost accountant can make effective use of work study information.

(IWSP *Costing Aspects*, 1973)

18. Define budgetary control and explain how it can assist a supervisor in his job.

(NEBSS Certificate, 1971)

19. What are the aims of work study?

(NEBSS Certificate, 1971)

20. Explain the difference between production and productivity.

(NEBSS Certificate, 1971)

21. Discuss the possible effects of increasing mechanization on the work of a supervisor.

(NEBSS Certificate, 1971)

2
The working basis of O and M

The very nature of O and M work, associated as it is with change, makes its place in the organization unique. Another of its special features in the organizational structure is its reporting line. O and M is a service to management and usually reports straight to a director in a manufacturing or commercial company. In a large local government authority the O and M officer may report directly to a Council committee, rather than to one of the council's professional officers, such as the town clerk or treasurer.

It is sometimes difficult for supervisors to understand the unusual position of O and M, particularly when presented with the apparent paradox of power, linked with a purely advisory nature. As it is vital for supervisors to understand the O and M function and co-operate with its personnel, an effort will be made in this chapter to explain the working basis of O and M and the supervisor's vital role.

2.1 The general place of O and M

The siting of O and M within the organization's structure is very important and care should be taken to locate it as effectively as possible. However, this is not the concern of the supervisor, but is a matter for top-level management, such as the board of directors, to decide. Figure 2.1 is part of the organization chart of a large manufacturing company, showing only three directors: production, management services, and personnel. This company has given serious thought to the role of management services and has put it in a strong setting, headed by a board director carrying the title of management services director. The portion of the chart at Figure 2.1 directly below this director is similar to Figure 1.4 (page 11), but observant readers will have noticed two additions. The first is the post of negotiator; he is a valuable supplement to a large management services department, involved as he inevitably will be in very large-scale negotiations. The second addition is that of a training section; this separate section is necessary to provide training for management services personnel and also for line managers, supervisors and other personnel affected by implementation of O and M proposals.

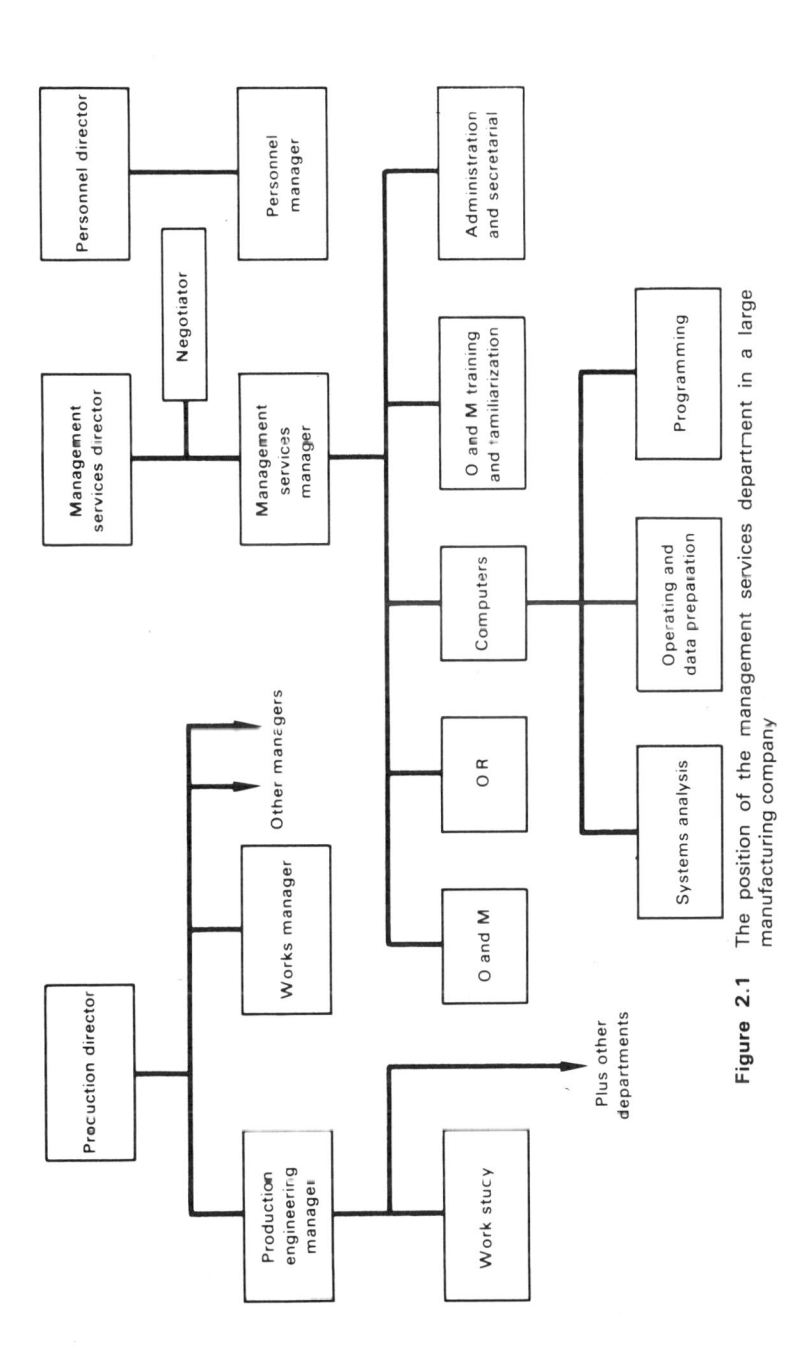

Figure 2.1 The position of the management services department in a large manufacturing company

The management services manager is seen to have three organizational relationships:

1. He is a line manager in his own right, with a line responsibility to his own personnel. That is to say, the specialists and other personnel in his own department report to him and to no one else. Their work is under his general direction: he alone is responsible to the management services director for the total management services effort.
2. Operationally, he is a purely functional manager and exists to give a service to conventional line managers, such as the works manager and the sales manager. It must be understood that the management services manager (and his professional staff) have a mainly persuasive role, as far as introducing methods changes is concerned.
3. After an O and M proposal has been accepted, O and M personnel may be allowed a temporary (implied) line authority during the implementation stages, because of their specialist knowledge of the machines and systems being introduced. In this case the management services manager also has a temporary (implied) line authority in a department other than his own. Where this works well, it usually does so due to the attractive and strong personality of the management services manager and his personnel.

2.2 Relationships with other departments

Now let us consider that part of the organization chart (Figure 2.1) which is outside the area of management services. Firstly, the area controlled by the production director: this board director has direct (line) control over a number of managers, two of which are shown on the chart, the works manager and the production engineering manager. Both of these have organizational collateral relationships with the management services manager.

The works manager has line control over and responsibility for the total direct-worker effort in the manufacturing area. Reporting to him are all the shop floor supervisors, although they may in fact report to a deputy works manager if the company is large. In fact, this company is so large that the board of directors decided to separate the highly specialized area of production engineering from the works management responsibility.

The production engineering manager, then, is responsible directly to the production director for such aspects as planning, estimating, tool design and manufacture, materials handling, plant layout, selection of new machinery and work study. The last-mentioned is of direct relevance to our discussion. First, it must be noted that the production engineering manager himself is a functional manager, giving a service to the works

The working basis of O and M

manager. In this case, it has been decided to place the responsibility for shop floor work study with this specialist engineering manager.

It is quite possible, indeed highly probable, that the production engineering manager would call on the assistance of the management services manager. Alternatively, the latter might wish to investigate the organization and methods of the former's department. In one actual case, known to the author, a production engineering manager and his team were planning a new factory and they called on the assistance of management services personnel to construct a critical path network for the new building. They also helped with a computer-assisted equipment ordering system.

Looking to the right of Figure 2.1, we see the post of personnel director. Reporting directly to him is the personnel manager, who is another functional (advisory) manager. The management services manager's relationship with the personnel manager is an organizational collateral relationship and he is therefore allowed and expected to work closely with the personnel manager without feeling the need to involve the two directors. There is a specially important relationship here as the working environment is inevitably changed by O and M recommendations.

The personnel manager is directly linked with such aspects of management services work as:
1. Recommendations influencing labour turnover
2. Plans for the training of personnel, including the training of O and M personnel
3. Plans for recruitment of new personnel, made necessary by O and M recommendations, and also new O and M personnel
4. Trades union negotiations concerning O and M recommendations

It can be seen that the management services department must work closely and in harmony with both line management and functional (service) departments. Their work is so closely knitted with the general activities of the organization that it is necessary to state the reasons for having a separate management services department. The main reasons are as follows:
1. The specialized and wide-ranging nature of the problems require the constant interchange of knowledge and creative thinking, which must be centralized if efficient use is to be made of such valuable labour.
2. If really effective methods changes are to be made, the management services department must be completely free from political and other pressures that might be present if they reported to a line manager.
3. A separate management services department can be objective and look at the organization from the detached point of view that is necessary for long-range creative thinking.

4. A central management services department can operate a strong training department for line personnel involved in O and M implementation and also O and M personnel. It can also provide a good training ground for line managers or potential managers as they spend short periods (say two or three years) as O and M officers.

Principles of organizational relationships concerning organization and methods will hold for any type of business, but the detailed outworkings will obviously bear the individual characteristics of the particular organization, be it industry, commerce, local government, central government or hospitals.

Local government is very big business, accounting for something like ten per cent of the national output. A large city could be employing in the region of 30 000 people, with a works department having a 'sales' turnover of over £6 million. To exercise control, local government officials need to apply management techniques in much the same way as business organizations. However, there is one essential difference. Management here is divided into two very distinct areas:

1. The policy-making council. This consists of part-time laymen, often unqualified in professional and management areas.
2. The professional chief officers and their staffs. This is further complicated by the fact that many chief officers have a split responsibility: on the one hand to the council and on the other hand to the government. A medical officer of health is an example.

Supervisors employed in local government will be interested to see a modern concept of the position of O and M in the local government organization structure (Figure 2.2) and it is hoped that other supervisors will be interested to compare the structure with their own organization. The new appointment of town manager is suggested in an effort to secure more efficient co-ordination of the work of departments employing large numbers of direct personnel and technical personnel. The town manager could be a promoted town clerk or a professional engineer or accountant. It can be seen that management services is part of the town manager's headquarters group and is closely linked with training, budgets, financial control and overall planning.

2.3 Relationships with trades unions

The management services manager's and O and M officer's relationship with the trades unions is particularly sensitive and difficult in the sense that there is no organizational relationship. Trades union representatives should participate as early and as continuously as possible, in an open and co-operative atmosphere, involving the personnel department at all stages. Senior management's policy on such important aspects as possible redundancies and transfer or dilution of jobs, should be obtained by the

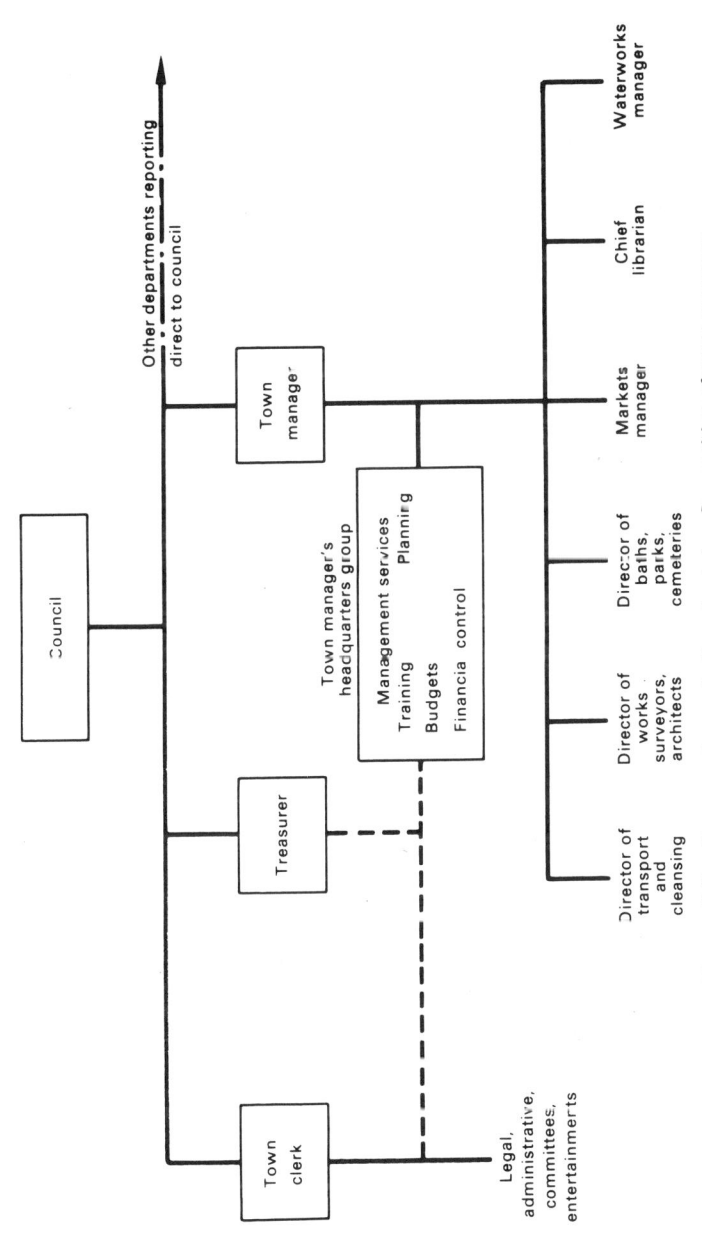

Figure 2.2 Suggested organization chart showing position of town manager

SOURCE 'The Organization of Local Government O and M, *Management in Action*, April 1971.

management services department through the personnel department, in the early stages, and discussed with the trades unions.

As ignorance inevitably breeds fear, the management services department should invite trades unions representatives to attend talks on the various management techniques that may be proposed for a particular investigation. They should receive a copy of the O and M report, or at least a copy of those sections dealing with matters directly affecting their members. Consultation at every stage is the key to good relationships between O and M personnel and the trades unions.

Figure 2.3 is an example of joint-consultation between a local government O and M department and the respective trades unions at the

---

Administration aspect commenced: ....

Operational aspect to commence: ....

This outline is prepared for the meeting of the O and M officer and trades union representatives.

Representatives in attendance from:
  NALGO, NUPE, NUGMW, TGWU

Outline of proposed procedure
1. Interviews with lay administrative officer (health dept.), ambulance officer and telephonists (ambulance depot).
2. Preparation of organization chart showing administrative and operational structure of the service. (Examination of lists of duties for all personnel.)
3. Examination of borough plan, noting positions of hospitals and other places of direct concern.
4. Examination of operational statistics available for the ambulance service.
5. Examination of equipment inventory associated with the service, including vehicles.
6. Interviews with drivers and attendants.
7. Activity studies on vehicles in the depot, day and night shifts.
8. Activity studies on vehicles outside the depot, day and night shifts.
9. Analysis of findings.
10. Draft report submitted to ambulance officer for his comments.
11. Final draft report submitted to medical officer of health for his comments.
12. Final report, submitted to medical officer of health for submittance by him to the health committee together with his comments.

Figure 2.3 Example of joint consultation before an O and M assignment in local government

commencement of an ambulance service O and M assignment (see *Report Writing for Supervisors* by the author, G. Bell and Sons Ltd., 1973). This was in a large county borough and there were several trades unions involved. Before starting the assignment the O and M manager held a meeting with their officials and incorporated some of their suggestions in the investigation.

2.4 Relationships with supervisors

Supervisors will normally become involved in O and M assignments at the following stages:
1. In preliminary interviews conducted by O and M specialists to ascertain the range of duties currently performed and the supervisor's understanding or interpretation of his role in the organization structure. Supervisors should prepare for such interviews and try to be as factual as possible.
2. Supervisors may be asked to take part in activity sampling exercises, including self-sampling. They should be as helpful as possible and ask to discuss the results of the analysis. Activity sampling normally takes the initial form of pilot studies and supervisors may be able to assist in the design of the main sampling programme.
3. During the main method study fact-gathering (recording) stage, supervisors can be particularly helpful in providing accurate information for the O and M specialists.
4. At the development stage of the O and M assignment, sweeping methods changes can be born and the supervisor should try to be involved with this work; he will be expected to work the new system long after the O and M specialists have moved on to new areas.
5. Supervisors should involve themselves closely with any work measurement exercises where an attempt is being made to create new standard times. The supervisor should ensure that shop stewards are kept in the picture.
6. In some cases supervisors may be able to influence the first stage in the O and M assignment, namely the selection stage. Although the main areas for study will have been selected by his manager and the management services or O and M manager, it can be a help to the O and M specialist and the supervisor himself, if he makes suggestions as to areas of study, based on his experience of the detailed work situation.
7. Supervisors may be asked to participate in proving trials of new machinery or procedures. They should be on the alert, maintaining a helpful but critical approach.
8. At the final stages of installation and maintenance, the supervisor's role becomes even more important. He must make sure that he thoroughly understands the new equipment and procedures and that his personnel understand them as well.

Although good relations are something at which to aim from the outset, such intentions do not always prevail, for a variety of reasons. For example, barriers such as the O and M specialist's use of management jargon or his higher educational level might intrude. The specialist also has a wider knowledge of overall procedures and the inter-relatedness of the work of different departments, and a greater experience of management techniques. He should endeavour to cause as little friction as possible, but much will also depend on the supervisor's own receptiveness, open-mindedness, level of management education and skill in communications. Supervisors who have obtained certificates and diplomas of the National Examinations Board in Supervisory Studies (NEBSS) and/or the Institute of Supervisory Management and the Institution of Works Managers, will be ideally placed to work closely with O and M specialists.

2.5 Management directives and the consultative role

The consultative nature of O and M in the setting of management directives is possibly one of the most puzzling aspects for the average supervisor. It may help if we consider one or two truisms, some linked with organizational concepts such as power (discussed in detail in the next chapter):

1. There are some things which you cannot force people to do.
2. The executive of an organization can instruct the O and M or management services manager to investigate a certain department or common service and can in fact instruct them to achieve a significant cost saving. However, this does not guarantee the achievement of the stated cost saving.
3. Continuing cost savings and improvements in efficiency and effectiveness will depend upon the fullest, continuing co-operation from line departments and all the personnel concerned.
4. The executive are also wasting their time merely instructing line managers and others to co-operate fully with O and M specialists. They must lead and set the example to subordinates. This point is mentioned here because the same rule applies to supervisors and their subordinates.

However, there should be no real problem over directives if the executive and the management carefully observe organizational principles. It is perfectly in order for the executive to instruct the O and M manager to undertake an investigation. The O and M manager will proceed in his functional role (providing a service to other line managers) to seek the assistance of a number of people in order to achieve the stated objectives. It is better if he is given an open instruction to report back on a practical solution to a problem after discussing it with line managers, and undertaking pilot studies. Of course, if this method is adopted, supervisors are involved in forming executive policy, which is in itself a valuable outcome.

Examination questions

1. There are varying reactions to the introduction of work study into an

The working basis of O and M

organization. What reactions would you expect from a supervisor and how would you deal with them?

(City & Guilds *Work Study*, 1968)

2. Does the practice of joint consultation create a better relationship between management and employees, or is it a waste of production time? Illustrate your answers with the key points to be borne in mind.

(IWSP Graduate *Industrial Relations*, 1969)

3. Discuss the conflicting loyalties that shop stewards may experience when carrying out their responsibilities.

(IWSP *Industrial Relations*, 1974)

4. A production manager states that he already has a rate-fixing department and asks why he should introduce work study. What answer would you give him?

(City & Guilds *Work Study*, 1974)

3
The study of organization

3.1 Purpose

The formal study of organization is peculiar to O and M work and is one of the major factors setting it apart from work study. Thus it is very important for supervisors studying O and M to grasp the principles of organization, which will also help them appreciate their role and achieve sound organizational relationships with their subordinates and management colleagues. In addition, the supervisor plays a leading part in his organization's first-line management and the higher his awareness of the structures in which he operates, the more successful will be his participation in the management activity.

A great deal of thought has been given to company organization structure since the American management pioneer F. W. Taylor (1856–1915) divided management activity into planning and performance and created management specialisms. Problems of industrial organization that were not previously isolated were then subjected to close investigation. A tremendous contribution was also made by Henri Fayol (1841–1925) through his work on general and industrial management, and such thinkers as Lyndall F. Urwick and E. F. L. Brech gave further assistance in shaping modern organizational theory.

In its simplest and most concise form, an efficient organization structure is a communications framework through which two-way information may pass. On the one hand it allows the executive to make its decisions known to the management and supervisors, including the shop floor and office floor where necessary, and on the other it encourages vital feedback from office and shop floor to management areas.

The organizational structure is concerned with facilitating the definition and allocation of work, and also its subsequent co-ordination.

3.2 Organizational definitions

Many phrases are loosely used in organizations, without serious thought being given to real meaning. It may be helpful to give more precise definitions of some of them here, since they have direct relevance to the work of the supervisor, involved as he should be in job descriptions and job development work for his subordinates.

A *duty* is an action which you ought to do or which you are compelled to do. In a company it is action and conduct due to a superior. Duties are allocated activities. In other words they are activities given to a man or woman to do.

Responsibility means that you are answerable to another for something. A shop floor or office supervisor will therefore be responsible to his superior for various duties which may include both allocated and unallocated activities. The latter category recognizes the fact that supervisors often carry out necessary work which has not been specifically given to them. The supervisor's or foreman's responsibility takes the form of reporting, personally or in written form, on the carrying out of his various duties and reporting on their completion. Real *authority* means the power or right to enforce obedience from others. It implies the ability or power to influence the conduct and actions of others. (We shall see later that power is an easily-used word, but the implementation of power is no easy matter.) In the most practical sense, as far as supervisors are concerned, authority gives them the right to use company resources such as equipment and supplies and the right to direct the work of their subordinates. However, the effectiveness of this direction will depend, in many situations, less on such factors as position in the company hierarchy and more on personality and personal example.

Supervisory authority in an organization can be subdivided into three different types. Firstly, there is personal authority, which is usually a result of a supervisor's obvious leadership qualities, arousing his subordinates' respect, or his seniority in the company hierarchy. Secondly, formal authority is the type of authority which is clearly delegated; for example, subordinates realize that a supervisor is passing on his manager's authority. It can also be legal authority, as in certain aspects of the work of safety officers and medical officers. Thirdly, functional authority is the type of authority which is based on specialized skills or knowledge. It is clearly in evidence when considering the roles of industrial chemists, work study officers, O and M officers and metallurgists, all of whom are personnel specifically hired to perform in their specialist areas.

The three other aspects of authority which concern us are line, functional and staff relationships, which are dealt with later in this chapter.

Supervisors, having been given considerable authority, must then accept *accountability* for the way in which they exercise their authority. They are liable to be called on to answer for their decisions and actions at any time.

Delegation is one of the most difficult methods of administration to achieve in management. It means sending or commissioning a person to act as your representative, often with power to act on your behalf, thus extending responsibility and also accountability. When a supervisor delegates, he assigns duties to his subordinates and grants authority to make commitments. This may include the right to give orders on his behalf. Delegation creates an obligation on the part of the subordinate to return a satisfactory performance of the duty.

In its absolute sense, *power* is the possession of control or command over others. It includes the ability to act or affect something strongly and often suggests force of character and physical or mental strength. In the management sense, a supervisor needs to have the capacity to change the behaviour of an individual or group of people for whom he is responsible. His real power lies in his leadership qualities.

Summary points. Although supervisors assign duties to their subordinates (delegation) and subsequently expect them to perform satisfactorily (obligation), they are not allowed to delegate their ultimate responsibility. When they accept authority, they also accept responsibility for the activities and behaviour of their subordinates and are accountable for successes and failures.

Supervisors and foremen in the modern industrial and commercial setting are in a difficult position and it is vital for them to understand the principles discussed, particularly in the areas of authority and power. Modern supervisors may wonder if they have any authority and power left, surrounded as they are by specialists such as personnel managers, work study managers, production engineers and O and M officers. However, if supervisors obtain a real understanding of modern organizational theory, they will realize that they can have more authority and power, in the truly satisfying sense, than supervisors in any past era.

3.3 Formal and informal organizational relationships

It is important to understand the different types of relationships which exist between groups of people in manufacturing organizations. We shall consider four formal relationships all of which will be seen in companies of any size. Figure 3.1 shows organizational relationships between some personnel in a manufacturing company. Readers should refer to this when reading the following definitions.

Line relationships. These are the direct relationships between supervisors and subordinates. The senior person has direct authority, although his responsibility is general. This means he has the executive right to expect his order to be obeyed by his men, but his responsibility is that of a general commanding: he does not claim to be, for example, a specialist in work study or metallurgy.

Functional relationships. Examples of functional specialists are O and M

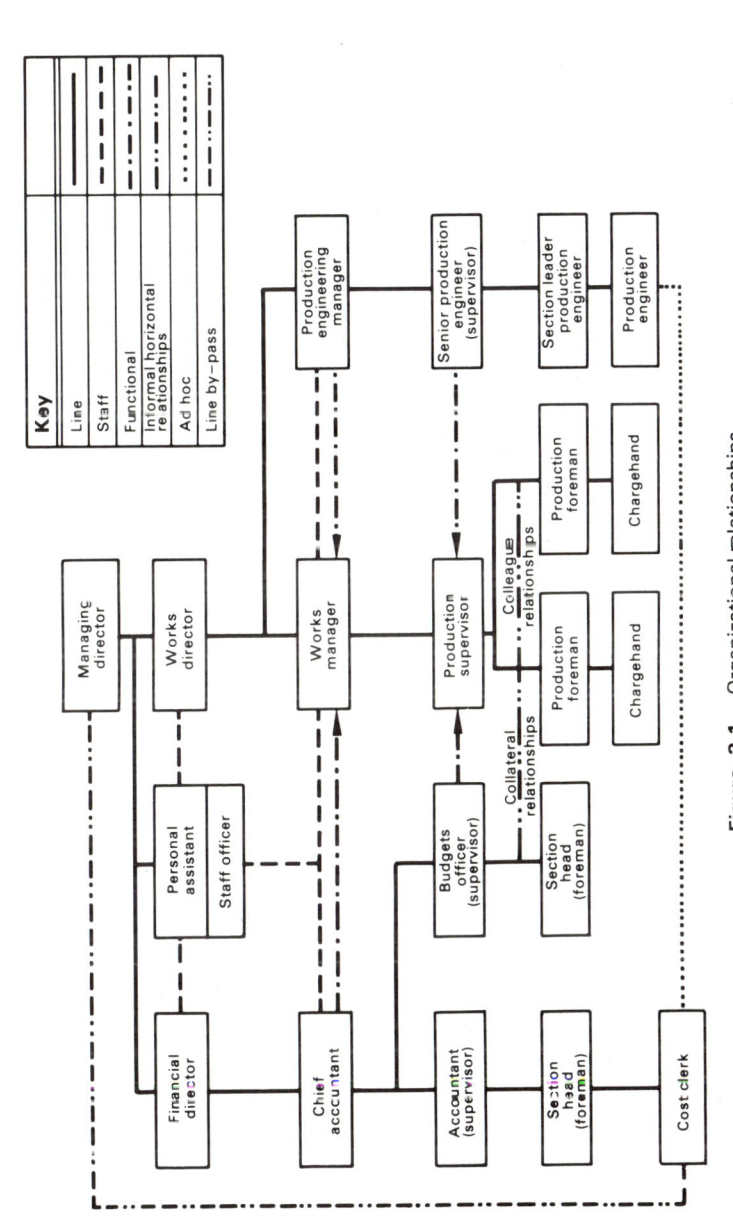

Figure 3.1 Organizational relationships

managers, production engineering managers, work study managers and their personnel. The functional specialist, when working outside his own department, only has indirect authority over the supervisor's or foreman's personnel, and he has a specialized responsibility. He is not a general commanding, but is only required to provide his specialized service.

After examining Figure 3.1 for functional relationships, the reader should examine Figure 3.2 which illustrates the influence of functional relationships in a very large manufacturing company. The production

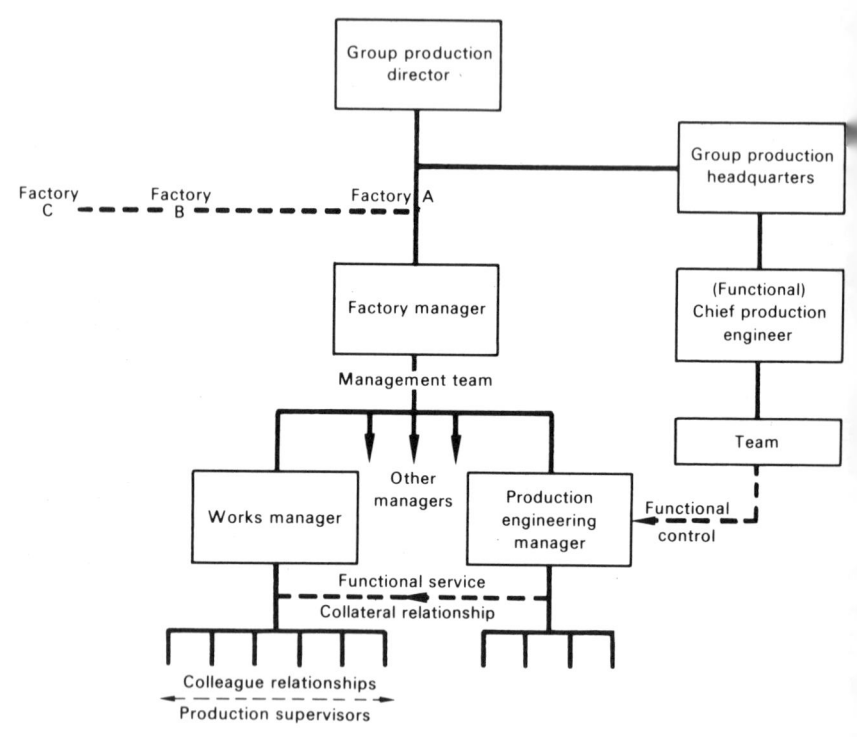

Figure 3.2 Extract from the organization chart of a very large manufacturing company, illustrating functional relationships

engineering manager is seen to be subject to two major influences, the line command from the factory manager and the functional command from the group chief production engineer. This arrangement can work very well in practice, providing that the production engineering manager remembers that his main loyalty and responsibility is to his immediate line manager, the factory manager.

The study of organization

The chief production engineer's (functional) group responsibility is to ensure that there are group policies on such aspects as standardization of production machinery and control equipment. Unless this is done, spare parts holding may be very high and there may also be problems over fixtures if machinery is re-grouped. The production superintendents and foremen will need to accept guidance from specialist production engineering personnel. The latter not only report to a different manager in their factory than the superintendents and foremen, but they are also under the influence of a chief production engineer who does not work in their factory at all. Office supervisors and section heads will also need to understand the similar organizational relationships with such specialists as O and M officers, sometimes going under the title of management services officers.

Staff relationships. Another feature of the large company is that, as well as employing functional specialists, the company may employ staff officers, for example a personal assistant to the managing director. The staff officer's authority is purely representative: he speaks only with permission of his chief and the requests and instructions he issues come, in reality, from his superior. His responsibility is purely advisory, but although the staff officer has no line or functional authority whatsoever, it would be foolish for a superior to be high-handed with a staff officer, or to ignore his requests.

Committee relationships. There is little point in arguing about the advisability of using committees in industrial management. The idea of attempting to run a sizeable undertaking today without committees is inconceivable. However, there are still plenty of managers who do not agree with committee organization; they are often the type of people who resent asking the opinions of others and also resent criticism.

Committee relationships can be tricky. Acrimony should be avoided whenever possible and much trouble can be avoided if a discussion is arranged before the formal committee meeting. Figure 3.3 attempts to give some idea of the complicated relationships that may exist in committee situations in a sizeable modern factory.

As well as the formal relationships of line, functional and staff, supervisors also need to understand some other organizational relationships which affect their work and role in the company organizational network of communications. In dealing with these informal relationships, we shall again make reference to Figure 3.1.

Horizontal relationships. These are sometimes referred to as lateral relationships. They concern relationships between personnel of equal authority and the same level of responsibility in the organization. Figure 3.1 shows two examples, in one case two production foremen and in the other a production foreman and a man of equivalent rank in the accounts department, the budgets section head. The first relationship is known as a (horizontal) colleague relationship; the second relationship is known as a

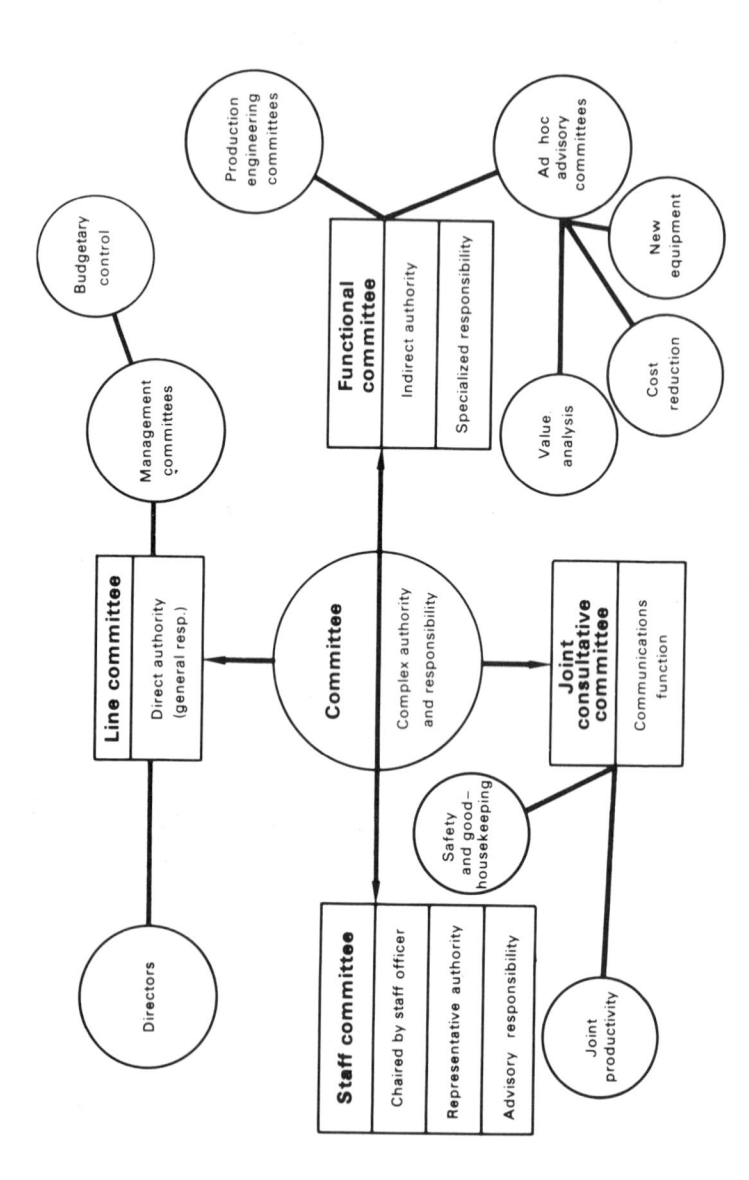

Figure 3.3 Committee relationships

(horizontal) collateral relationship. These relationships may be described as communications bridges and that is precisely their function.

Ad hoc relationships. These are informal relationships on numerous and varied day-to-day matters between rank and file personnel from different departments. Since they do not necessarily include their respective superiors, they can achieve great savings in time. However, these personnel must remember that they are not allowed to commit their superiors on policy or other important matters without previously referring to them. Sometimes such a relationship can manifest itself in the form of a small informal committee meeting.

Line by-pass relationships. One such relationship is shown in Figure 3.1: other examples occur when the managing director goes directly to a production chargehand, operative or office worker for some information without informing the person's superior. This situation may often result in an instruction being given, which is, in many instances, a very unsatisfactory procedure. Nevertheless, managers and supervisors will doubtless meet this practice.

The most obvious reason for a senior person to take such action would be if the foreman and other senior manufacturing personnel were absent from their offices or areas and the matter was urgent. However, there may be many other reasons: information may be becoming distorted on its way up the line organization communications network; the managing director may not be satisfied with the service that he is receiving; the area concerned may not be responding to decisions as he would wish; the people concerned may not be clear on their duties and responsibilities. It will be noted that these situations could, and should, be put right by attention to organizational weaknesses.

Extending the scope of the relationships discussed, those responsible for others should observe the following code if they wish to observe good organizational procedures.

Subordinates

1. Subordinates should have a clear set of duties and responsibilities and they should be given authority to carry them out.
2. Instructions should not be given direct to a subordinate's staff and certainly not in the absence of the subordinate, unless there are exceptional circumstances.
3. The supervisor should wherever possible avoid entering a subordinate's working area without first contacting the subordinate. If an inspection tour is intended, the subordinate should accompany the supervisor.
4. If possible, advance warning should be given of an intended visit; he or she may wish to prepare a progress report to make the tour more worthwhile and factual.
5. Discovery of departmental inefficiency is less likely to be achieved by

random, unannounced visits than by inviting a work study officer to undertake an assignment.
6. Supervisors should obtain the fullest communication and cooperation without causing any confusion or bad feeling.

Superiors
1. A progress summary should be kept available for the manager, noting in particular progress made on key jobs.
2. Any management memos and questionnaires must be answered in good time.
3. If the supervisor has to be absent from his department to go to some other part of the organization, a note should be left saying where he is.
4. Before leaving the factory or building, permission must first be obtained from the manager.
5. The supervisor should ensure that he is well briefed by his subordinates before attending a management meeting.
6. The manager should be kept closely in touch with office or shop-floor feeling and attitudes.
7. Managers should be constantly supplied with cost reduction ideas.

3.4 Company organizational structure

The following outline of company organizational structure will be of direct relevance to supervisors employed in manufacturing companies. Supervisors in other organizations, such as local government, should look for similar aspects of their own organizations.

The organizational structure of a company is a framework for executive and management decision-making. Organization is concerned with the grouping of activities, assignment of activities and the provision for authority, delegation and co-ordination. Necessary activities are subdivided and arranged in groups which may be assigned to individuals according to their duties and responsibilities.

The main divisions of a modern industrial enterprise of reasonable size are product design development, marketing, manufacturing, finance, administration, personnel, purchasing and management services.

The three stages of planning. A sound company organizational structure will be linked with the three stages of policy planning, general management planning and planning of actual manufacturing. General management planning is expressed in the accurate preparation and implementation of the interconnected and related budgets covering manufacturing, sales and marketing, purchasing, personnel and administration, financial, research and development, and distribution. Overall budgetary control can then be operated to give the intended systematic control of business operations through budgets carrying such

The study of organization

titles as sales, production (including plant and equipment), materials, labour, works expense (indirect factory charges) and financial.

Higher control. This is a monthly survey of the functional activities of the business, based on comparison of the present position with that at the end of the last financial year. It summarizes the trading position and the financial position.

3.5 Principles of organization

The following 12 principles of organization should be studied by supervisors, for application to their own jobs and also to be borne in mind when discussing the work of others. As with all principles, they should form guidelines for action.

1. *The unity of objective.* All should contribute harmoniously to the achievement of the common good of the business and the individual members of the business. The common good includes primary objectives such as producing and selling goods of the required quality (and creating the planned profit) and collateral objectives such as job satisfaction and the payment of wages. Good communications and joint consultation are required.

2. *The scalar principle.* Formal authority, or rank, is necessary in the company and lines of authority should be clearly designated and understood by all personnel concerned.

3. *The principle of correspondence.* The modern supervisor should be given responsibility and he should be trained to accept this responsibility. He must then take the credit or blame for the outcome of his actions (sharing accountability). It is not always easy to pinpoint responsibility in the correct quarter in some factories, but this is often due to a poor inspection and quality control system. For example, poor quality materials are issued to machine shops and the blame for poor workmanship and excess costs may be directed at the wrong supervisor by an unselective accountancy procedure.

Authority implies the right to use resources of manufacturing and accountability implies answerability for the way in which a supervisor exercises his authority.

4. *Delegation.* Authority to carry out work should be passed down as far as possible in the organization. This is the modern approach in management and supervisors should involve as many of their personnel as possible in the team objectives.

5. *Unity of command.* Each person should only receive instructions from one superior. However, supervisors need to understand the role of functional specialists such as inspectors, quality control engineers, production engineers and management services personnel. These people can assist the supervisor in his daily work, but their initial approach to his

department should always be through him and he should be kept fully informed of their activities.

6. *Span of control.* In any situation there will be a maximum number of direct subordinates over whom a supervisor can effect proper control, if the work of the subordinates is interconnected. The number ranges from around 5 to 7, depending upon the complexity of the operation.

Factors which help to decide on the controllable span include: the efficiency of communications in the company; distance between the departments concerned; the type of work, for example its complexity; the quality of personnel; the extent of delegation intended.

7. *The principle of specialization.* Specialization is to be encouraged, since it results in increased human dexterity, reduced loss of time due to not having to continually change from one type of work to another, and the use of specialized machinery. However, the modern supervisor should be aware of the sociologist's warnings here. Loss of skills and soundly-based pride can lead to deterioration of valuable morale and greatly diminished efficiency.

8. *Discipline.* An efficient organization requires discipline if work is to be carried out to acceptable quality and safety standards and in accordance with production requirements. Discipline implies mutually-accepted environmental rules where well-defined duties are carried out without unnecessary pressure. Modern supervisors will realize that they should set an overall example to their subordinates and discipline should be implied in an environment of motivation.

9. *Fair rewards.* Most people respond to rewards. Although financial rewards are the first to come to mind when considering work which has been well done, there are many other effective means of indicating satisfaction. Some of these will be dictated by company policy, but supervisors should try to ensure that personnel receive adequate incentives.

10. *Effective centralization.* A planned amount of centralization is necessary: for example, there are good reasons for having centralized personnel and accountancy functions. In very large companies, headquarters staff departments such as production engineering can implement an overall policy on equipment purchasing for a number of factories, ensuring, for example, standardization of control equipments and avoidance of spare parts difficulties.

11. *Justice and fair play.* It is worth remembering the precept that justice should not only be done, but should be seen to be done. Supervisors should not make rash personal promises, or make promises involving company policy without first consulting higher management. Once a promise has been made, it should be kept.

12. *Minimum labour turnover.* A manufacturing supervisor or foreman should aim to keep labour turnover in his department to a minimum. In this way the company will gain the maximum benefit from personnel

The study of organization 35

training programmes, the cost of recruiting new labour will be minimized and morale will be improved. The burden of the supervisor will also be lightened.

3.6 Company size

Size is no guarantee of efficiency and many small firms are as efficient and as profitable as large companies. Size in itself may not even ensure lower prices through the hoped-for economies of large-scale production.

Although there is a marked trend towards the grouping of business ownership and small companies are being swallowed up by larger companies, there will not necessarily be a dramatic reduction in the number of manufacturing units. In fact, the soundness of the theory of larger and larger production units is being challenged by management thinkers. It is suggested that around 750 to 1000 employees represents the maximum number which can be well-managed as a single unit although other factors, such as location and complexity of product or process, may influence any arithmetical calculation.

The total number of manufacturing establishments in the UK is listed at almost 92 000 (91 788) in the *Annual Abstract of Statistics* (1972) and around 30 000 of these only employ between one and ten personnel. The total number of personnel is around eight millions (7 826 000). However, such figures taken on their own give a misleading impression and Figure 3.4 gives an analysis of the statistics for the UK mechanical engineering industry, as an example. Establishments employing 500 or more employees account for nearly fifty per cent of the total number of employees in the industry. Supervisors in these establishments will inevitably be involved in complex organizational and communications problems.

Businesses often start from quite humble beginnings and the organization chart of Figure 3.5 shows the development of a small manufacturing company started by two partners, after it has grown to the stage where it employs a total of 50 personnel. One partner is looking after the sales side of the business, leaving the other partner to concentrate on the manufacturing side. There is only one foreman, who is responsible for 35 production workers and two tooling maintenance workers: from the organization chart, it can be seen that the foreman reports directly to a partner. This foreman is clearly in the favourable position of receiving instructions straight from a director and he is also in sole charge of the shop floor manufacturing operation. There are no other management personnel who can legitimately interfere in his area. He has a large say in the recruitment and selection of shop floor workers and is responsible for the quality of the work produced, as well as setting any standards for a 'fair day's work' (work standards). The loading of

	Analysis by number of employees							
	1–10	11–24	25–99	100–499	500–999	1000–1499	1500 or more
Approximate percentage of total number of establishments	38.3	28.2	18.7	11.3	2.1	0.6	0.8
			96.5%				
Approximate percentage of total number of employees	2.5	5.9	12.4	30.0	17.3	9.7	22.2
			50.8%				

SOURCE: *Annual Abstract of Statistics*, 1972.

Notes: 1. Total establishments 12 988.
2. As this figure was increased from 11 625 by the statistical office in order to compensate for unsatisfactory returns during the census, the latter figure is used here in calculating percentages to ensure accuracy.

Figure 3.4 UK mechanical engineering industry establishments

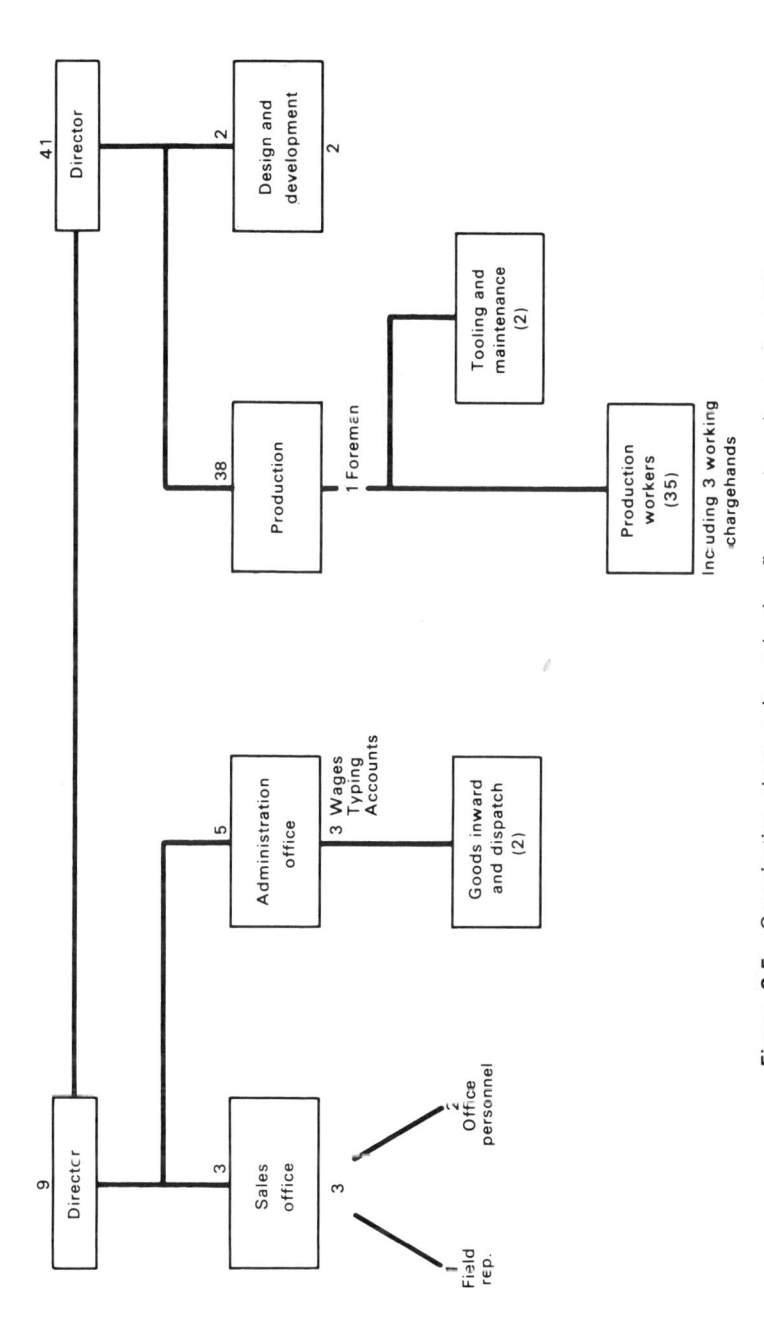

Figure 3.5 Organization chart: unit production firm employing a total of 50 personnel

work into manufacturing is also his responsibility, as well as some purchasing of tools and materials.

If the same company developed to a point where the number employed was 200, the number of directors could increase to four and specialist functions such as personnel and production engineering could be introduced. The foreman could then become just one of five production foreman, or he might be promoted to production superintendent, reporting to a works manager. Functions such as tool planning, ordering, work standards, maintenance, shop loading, quality and recruitment would then have passed into the hands of other management personnel.

If this seems appalling to our foreman, what will he think of the next stage in the company's development, shown by the organization chart at Figure 3.6. The company now employs 1000 personnel. One director has now been charged with overall responsibility for steering company policy and has the title of managing director. The number of directors is now five and there is a seven-strong senior management team, comprising sales manager, chief accountant, works manager, production engineering manager, chief engineer, personnel manager, purchasing manager and management services officer.

In practice, the type of organizational structure will vary according to the type and complexity of the business conducted and in the organization at Figure 3.6 separate financial and purchasing functions have been set up. Production engineering has now been strengthened and is headed up by a production engineering manager. The foremen and superintendents are not shown on the chart, but in fact they have become more important.

The biggest changes noticed by our foreman concern the introduction of specialist functions headed by specialist managers. It is vitally important for the manufacturing supervisor or foreman to understand the more complex type of organization outlined here.

3.7 Company type

For the purposes of this discussion we shall use five categories of manufacturing: unit production; batch production; flow production; batch/flow production; process production. The term mass production is not included here, since it is merely production on a large scale, which may be achieved by unit, batch or flow production methods. ('Large-scale' is not meant to imply large in physical size, but large-quantity production.) The expression unit production is used in preference to job production. There is an unfortunate linking of the latter expression with what is known as jobbing production, which is usually meant to imply any work carried out against a specific customer's order.

Unit production. In this type of production a single product, which is often a large, special-purpose machine, is built by a team of workers. The

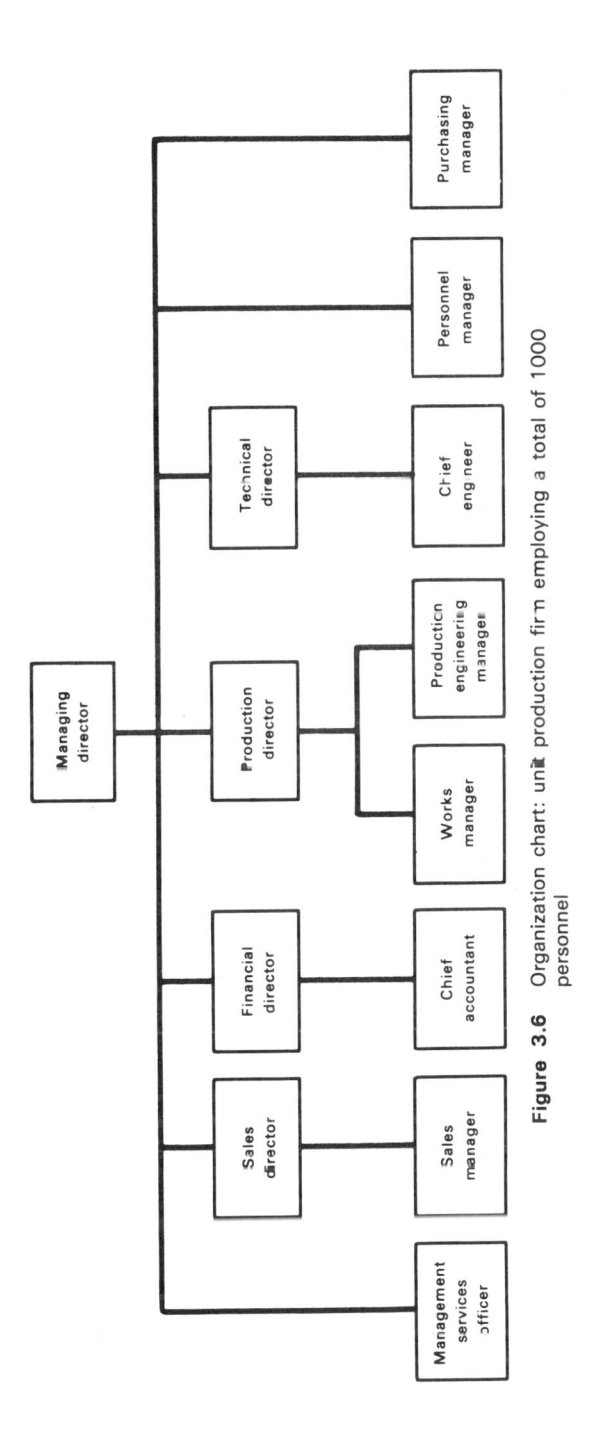

Figure 3.6 Organization chart: unit production firm employing a total of 1000 personnel

identifying feature of unit production is that the machine or other unit under consideration is regarded as a single operation and one product is completed before the team moves on to the next product. Unit production is well suited to the production of both simple units made to a customer's order and also technically complex units.

Batch production. This production method is normally used when a company is required to make a number or batch of identical units, where the work on each unit is divided into elements or parcels of work. Batch production is thus a natural outcome of the principle of elemental breakdown in work study. Each element is completed for the whole batch of units before proceeding to the next element. For example, if we are building ten machines for a customer and each machine has one large drive shaft, a lathe operator would be given a batch of ten drive shafts to machine. There could be many other operations to be performed on this shaft and the whole batch of ten shafts would move from stage to stage until completed. In batch production it is common to see the grouping of machines together: so in this example, all the lathes would be grouped.

Batch production is very common in Great Britain and it has the clear advantage of specialization of labour. However, problems arise with work-in-progress due to differences in work (time) content; in-process buffer (safety) stocks thus become a feature of this system. Sound production control is required in order to avoid unnecessary build-ups in work-in-progress with the associated tying up of cash.

Flow production. In this method, work is passed through the production process in strict operation sequence, allowing the best advantage to be taken of floor space and specialized machinery. It is important, therefore, to reduce queueing between operations and work-in-progress to a minimum. Examples of products which are suitable for flow production are motor cars and domestic appliances such as electric irons and washing machines. However, it should be noted that serious financial problems can arise from poor supervision of this method, leading to plant shutdown and materials shortages, not to mention possible labour troubles which are especially dangerous due to the dependence of one part of the flow line on the others.

Batch/flow production. Many large companies use a combination of batch and flow production. In the manufacture of motor cars, for example, the main production flow lines are fed with batch-produced units, such as engines and axle assemblies.

Process production. There is a sense in which process production may be considered as a form of flow production. However, it has been separated under a special heading here, because this type of industry has special problems for the manufacturing supervisor or foreman which are not always appreciated. Companies using this method of production (often manufacturing chemicals in batches or a continuous flow of liquid bases and solids) usually have a high intensity of investment in plant and often

The study of organization

use a nucleus of highly trained personnel, such as industrial chemists, and a work force of unskilled or semi-skilled plant operators. Plant maintenance and safety considerations become very important and the supervisor's role is a vital one.

3.8 Centralization and decentralization

Although centralization is usually taken to mean the bringing together of various functions in one location, it can also imply, in certain cases, that the authority that was once delegated is withdrawn. Conversely, if a procedure or process is decentralized, an organization needs to consider just what level of decision-making may be passed out of the hands of higher management. Thought must also be given in this situation to the monitoring procedures which are required to ensure that control is still in the hands of higher management, and the special training and recruitment programmes that are needed.

We may consider two types of decentralization.

Functional decentralization. In this type, special manufacturing units may be set up in a large company to handle one area of the company's work, such as castings, forgings, sheet metal work, assembly work, plastics. In one very large engineering company, for example, all castings are manufactured at a precision casting facility: some companies call them work centres. These centres are usually totally self-accounting and in effect 'sell' their products to the area of the company requiring them. The main advantage of this type of organization is the concentration of specialized knowledge and experience possible. Some people argue that it only produces more and more people knowing more about less and less. It is certainly important to take steps that such personnel do not lose sight of overall company objectives and forget that others have problems which they could help to solve.

Federal decentralization. In this type, special manufacturing units may be set up to handle a complete, finished product or products: for example, one factory may manufacture and market electric irons and toasters. One of the obvious disadvantages of such an organization is that it really creates a number of completely independent businesses in the company, with the great danger of isolationism, but there is also the clear advantage that the management efficiency of the teams controlling such separate units can be completely judged on their results.

Supervisors starting their careers in small companies will find themselves in a centralization environment. If they stay with a rapidly growing company or move to a large, actively diversifying company, they may find decentralization taking place. In this case they could become completely self-accounting for their responsibility, which might be the finest training possible for an ambitious supervisor.

3.9 Manuals and responsibility charts

Progressive organizations raise documents for key jobs and sometimes for all jobs, describing such features as: detailed description of the job, including a statement of duties and responsibilities, and degree of authority; organization charts of different departments of the company, including overall company organization charts; descriptions of salary scales, where the policy is to publish them. These documents are conveniently grouped together in an organization manual and supervisors should make themselves conversant with it. It is obvious that if a supervisor is being interviewed by an O and M practitioner who is compiling such a manual, he should give as much factual information to the O and M specialist as possible. Such manuals are also helpful when preparing job development and Management by Objectives (MBO) programmes.

Responsibility charts are visual aids used by O and M practitioners to find out some facts relating to organizational relationships and responsibilities. According to the strict organizational principles discussed in this chapter, some of these charts might be better described as duty charts or duty and responsibility charts.

Figure 3.7 shows an extract from a responsibility chart. Supervisors could benefit from drawing up a similar chart for their own departments.

Examination questions

1. Give three factors which help to determine how many subordinates a particular supervisor can directly control.
   (NEBSS Certificate, 1970)
2. What is meant by span of control in an organization structure?
   (NEBSS Certificate, 1969)
3. Explain the term line organization and illustrate your answer with a simple sketch of a chart.
   (NEBSS Certificate, 1969)
4. What is the essential difference between delegation and the giving of instructions?
   (NEBSS Certificate, 1970)
5. What symptoms would cause a works manager to consider that there is too little effective delegation within his sphere of responsibility? What are the principal problems to be overcome in achieving effective delegation?
   (IWM *Works Management Theory & Practice*)
6. What are the factors on which the correct span of control would depend?
   (IWSP *Associated Techniques*, 1968)
7. Why is feedback an essential part of any control system?
   (NEBSS Certificate, 1970)

Department	Invoice checking office	Supervisor		Mr. A. Jenkins
Aspect	Supervisor	Senior clerk	Calculating machine operator	Clerk/typist	Office junior
Opening mail					Opens and sorts invoices
Goods received notes					Sorts GR notes
Invoices/ GR notes				Marries together	
Invoice checking		Examines major discrepancies	Spot checks	Checks s-totals and totals	
Checked invoices		Checks summary sheets		Checks groupings, types summary sheets	Takes to accounts/ payments section
Price lists			Up-dates lists	Types new lists	
Progress reports		Prepares and submits, weekly		Types reports	
Communication with suppliers		Letters and visits (to major suppliers)	Telephone	Types letters	In envelopes and franking

Figure 3.7 Extract from a responsibility chart for an invoice checking office

8. Comment on the importance of colleague and collateral relationships to the practising production foreman or office section leader.
9. What are the objectives of a joint consultative committee and in what areas can the committee be effective in an industrial establishment?
(IWSP *Industrial Relations*, 1972)
10. (i) Prepare a typical organization chart for a manufacturing company employing 1000 people.
   (ii) What is the purpose of an organization chart?
   (iii) What benefits can be derived from preparing and interpreting such a chart?
(IWSP *Associated Techniques A*, 1972)
11. Explain what is understood by:
   (i) job production

(ii) flow production
　　　(iii) batch production
　　What are the limitations of these types of production?
　　　　　　　　　　　　　　　(IWSP *Business Organization*, 1974)
12.　(i) What is the source of a manager's authority?
　　　(ii) Discuss the need for delegation and the conditions for making it effective.
　　　　　　　　　　　　(Institution of Works Managers, college paper)
13.　What do you think of the suggestion that committees in industry are seldom worth their trouble and very often result in conflict and friction rather than co-ordinated action?
　　　　　　　　　　　　(Institution of Works Managers, college paper)
14.　Discuss the nature of delegation. Explain the practical difficulties of delegation and the steps that can be taken to make it more effective.
　　　　　　　　　　　　(Institution of Works Managers, college paper)
15.　Define the various characteristics of job, batch and flow production.
　　　　　　　　　　　　(Institution of Works Managers, college paper)
16.　List the duties of a work study practitioner within an organization.
　　　　　　　　　　　　　　　(City & Guilds *Work Study*, 1974)
17.　Explain the following types of relationship within an organization:
　　　(i) line
　　　(ii) staff
　　　(iii) functional
　　　　　　　　　　　　　　　　　　(NEBSS Certificate, 1971)

4
Applied work study principles—the standard time

Work study was defined in Chapter 1, but some repetition here will be directly useful in considering the following pages.

Work study. This is a management service, based on those techniques, particularly method study and work measurement, which are used in the examination of human work in all its contexts, and which lead to the systematic investigation of all the resources and factors which affect the efficiency and economy of the situation being reviewed, in order to effect improvement.

Method study. We define this as a systematic recording and critical examination of the factors and resources involved in existing and proposed ways of doing work, as a means of developing and applying easier and more effective methods and reducing costs.

Work measurement. This is the application of techniques designed to establish the time for a qualified worker to carry out a specified job at a defined level of performance.

If supervisors are to be effective, they must understand the principles and procedures of work study, a subject that is fundamental to the whole philosophy of management techniques. In this chapter we shall discuss practical aspects of work study, which will be particularly useful to supervisors undertaking project report writing required by examining bodies such as the National Examinations Board in Supervisory Studies (NEBSS) and the Institution of Works Managers (IWM). (See also the author's book *Report Writing for Supervisors*, G. Bell & Sons Ltd., 1973.)

4.1 Work study procedure

There is a definite and logical thought-process fundamental to the work study approach to problem investigation and the eight-stage procedure is given below. Supervisors are not expected to follow this procedure slavishly, but to adapt it to suit their particular problem situations.

Stage 1: select and define. At this initial stage a suitable problem should be chosen, defined and studied. Some use of method study and work measurement may be necessary here if a sound selection is to be made.

Stage 2: record. Facts should be recorded from direct observation, using method study and work measurement. It is a golden rule of work study that as much as possible of a study should be based on personal observation and not on second- or third-hand information. At this stage all the relevant (and seemingly relevant) facts should be recorded, since it is not possible to know in advance just which facts will be pertinent to the study in question. If facts are gathered rigorously and are well documented, they can be easily sifted when the development stage is reached.

Stage 3: examine. It is now necessary to critically examine the recorded facts. This must be done fairly, objectively and impartially. There is a procedure to help in this process, known as critical examination and this will be discussed shortly. Method study and work measurement may again be useful.

There is no reason to work in isolation on a work study investigation; others should be encouraged to contribute to all stages of the procedure. In this way, there is more likelihood of a sound and acceptable proposal being put forward.

Stage 4: develop. This is the all-important, creative stage of the procedure and it is not given to everyone to be creative. If the person undertaking the work study investigation cannot convince himself at this stage that he has discovered a better way of doing the job, then he must be honest about it and withdraw. It is vital to remember that we are concerned here with developing a new and better method, not just a replacement for the current state of affairs. The onus is on the supervisor to prove that the new method *is* a better one. Method study is used here.

Stage 5: measure. This stage is really integral with Stage 4, since it involves measuring the work content of the proposed (better) method or methods. It is preferable if one or two alternatives can be presented to management, in order that they are not faced with a 'take it or leave it' solution. Standard times are calculated at this stage and work measurement is used.

Stage 6: define. Now the new (better) methods must be clearly defined, in writing, together with the related times.

Presuming that the work study report is accepted by management, probably in a modified form, the next stages follow automatically, but a work specification should be written, particularly if we are dealing with a major shop floor study. This will be discussed later.

Stage 7: (acceptance and) install. At this stage we install the (accepted) better method, to be implemented as future agreed standard practice. Method study knowledge and practice is used here. 'Acceptance' has been added to the 'install' stage because it is vital to ensure that the acceptance of the new method by any affected employee, manager or group of

Applied work study principles—the standard time 47

employees is not merely a reluctant or non-cooperative acquiescence. In some companies, a foreman or supervisor may well be expected to install his 'better method', so it is imperative for him to make sure that his recommendations are valid and also to spend time in discussion with key people. The central core of the work study procedure is accurate facts. The examination of these facts, critically, leads to the development of better methods.

Stage 8: maintain. Once introduced, new methods must be maintained, lest people slip back into their old, familiar ways of doing work. The new work standards must therefore be protected by using control procedures. Method study may be used here, although cost accountancy can often provide real control, through its reporting-back procedure.

4.2 Critical examination

Critical examination is 'the systematic analysis of information about a problem, process, procedure or activity, by which it is subjected to exhaustive questioning and criticism' (British Standard 3138: 1969). The questioning technique is thorough and exhaustive and falls into two distinct sections.

Primary questions. Fundamental questions are asked regarding each activity, concerning: the need (purpose) for it; the place, the sequence; the person; its means. It is vital to challenge the need first, as often an activity is found to be unnecessary. For example, in O and M work it is pointless to design sophisticated filing systems for a department if the department does not have any use for the documents. 'Sequence' does not refer to the time of day but the relationship with other activities; for example, 'parcel wrapping takes place after component leaves assembly line, after stamping and inspection'. An example of 'means' could be 'parcel is wrapped by hand and tied with string'.

Secondary questions. The remaining essential activities must now be subjected to further questioning in order to discover alternatives and select those which are considered to be practicable and preferable. For example, 'How else could it be done?', 'How should it be done?'

O and M and work study practitioners normally use a form to assist with critical examination and a blank is shown as Figure 4.1, suitably annotated.

Figure 4.2 shows a simple example of a completed critical examination form, pointing out the type of answers required. For example, in the section 'What is achieved?', students often write something like 'The component is wrapped in paper and tied with string'. However, this statement does not supply the requisite information, although it is factually correct; the achievement is that the parcel is protected and that is the required specification.

Applied work study principles—the standard time

METHOD STUDY: (Critical Examination)
Study Ref.:

	STAGE I		STAGE II	
			Primary Questions	Secondary Questions / Selected Alternatives
PURPOSE (need)	What is achieved?	Why is it done?	What else could be done?	What should be done?
PLACE	Where is it done?	Why there?	Where else could it be done?	Where should it be done?
SEQUENCE	When is it done?	Why then?	When else could it be done?	When should it be done?
PERSON	Who does it?	Why that person?	Who else could do it?	Who should do it?
MEANS	How is it done?	Why that way?	How else could it be done?	How should it be done?
	PRIMARY QUESTIONS		SECONDARY QUESTIONS	SELECTED ALTERNATIVES

Figure 4.1 Critical examination

Applied work study principles—the standard time

METHOD STUDY: (Critical Examination)

Study Ref.: PARCEL WRAPPING (LIGHT COMPONENTS)

	What is achieved?	Why is it done?	What else could be done?	What should be done?
PURPOSE (need)	Component is protected	Specification states that 'goods should be protected and securely fastened'	Nothing	Product must still be protected in some way
PLACE	Where is it done? Parcel room	Why there? At end of production line and near to despatch bay	Where else could it be done? On production line itself	Where should it be done? At end of production line (on the actual line)
SEQUENCE	When is it done? After component leaves assembly line, after stamping and inspection	Why then? Always done that way. Must follow stamping and inspection	When else could it be done? No other process sequence time acceptable	When should it be done? No change, except before leaving line
PERSON	Who does it? Male packers	Why that person? Always done that way	Who else could do it? Female packers	Who should do it? Female packers (on production line)
MEANS	How is it done? Wrapped by hand and tied with string	Why that way? Always done that way (but see spec. above)	How else could it be done? Supplying special padded bags, stapling open ends	How should it be done? Bag dispenser and semi-automatic stapling machine at end of production line

Figure 4.2 Critical examination, parcel wrapping

4.3 The standard time

As mentioned earlier, one of the most significant contributions made by work study to management efficiency is the setting of standards. Amongst the more important of these is the labour standard, which is an evaluation of the work content or amount of work in a task. Work study seeks to establish the work content in standard units of time, such as standard hours or minutes. The standard time is thus the total time in which a job should be completed at standard performance: it is made up of the work content (total), plus the work contingency allowance and delay contingency allowance where applicable. (Standard performance is the rate of output which qualified workers will naturally achieve without over-exertion as an average over the working day or shift, provided they adhere to the specified method and are motivated to apply themselves to their work.)

After the best method of carrying out the work is discovered by the use of method study, the standard time may be established by the use of work measurement. Figure 4.3 shows the build up of a standard time, in diagrammatic form. Supervisors must have a thorough understanding of this and we shall work through the diagram, from left to right.

Total work content				
Basic work content				
Selected basic time	Relaxation allowance		Work contingency allowance	Delay contingency allowance
	Fatigue	Personal		
Standard time				

Selected basic time = selected observed time × $\dfrac{\text{observed rating}}{\text{standard rating}}$

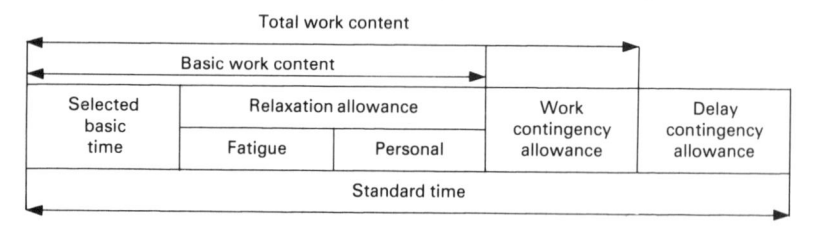

Figure 4.3 Build up of standard time

Selected basic time. The first step in work measurement is to record the observed times for a number of repetitive cycles of the task. The observed time is 'the time taken to perform an element or combination of elements obtained by means of direct measurement' (British Standard 3138: 1969). (Later in this chapter we shall discuss the process of deciding on the number of cycles to record, and other related technical aspects.)

The effective time is then identified, being that portion of the elapsed (watch) time during which the worker is engaged in the proper performance of the prescribed task. It is at this stage that we must consider the concept of rating, bearing in mind that it is necessary to judge whether the observed worker fits into the definition of a representative worker, laid down as 'a worker whose skill and performance is the average of a group under consideration'. In short, we

Applied work study principles—the standard time 51

must adjust the effective (observed) time to bring the effort to a reference point representing a performance achievable by an 'average' worker. This is done by making mental reference to an international scale of performance rating, described in the next section.

Performance rating. To rate is to assess a worker's rate of working relative to an observer's concept of the rate corresponding to standard rating. Standard rating is the rating corresponding to the average rate at which a qualified worker will naturally work, provided he keeps to the specified method and is motivated to apply himself to the work.

Figure 4.4 gives a table of ratings on the British Standard 0/100 Scale, to give a rough idea of the concept of rating.

British standard rating	Comments on performance	Comparative walking speed (m.p.h.)
50	Very slow, clumsy, 'half-asleep', no interest	2
75 Normal rating	Steady: deliberate, unhurried, under proper supervision: looks slow, but time not wasted under observation	3*
100 Standard rating	Brisk, businesslike performance: average trained worker under incentive conditions; achievement with confidence	4
125	Very fast: high degree of assurance, dexterity and co-ordination: well above-average performance for a trained worker	5
150	Exceptionally fast: intense effort and concentration. Virtuoso performance. Only achieved by a few outstanding workers	6

SOURCE: Adapted from International Labour Office Handbook *Introduction to Work Study*.

* Note: The speed of motion of the limbs of a man of average physique walking without load in a straight line on level ground. (Europeans and North Americans working in temperate conditions.) Another guide is to deal a pack of fifty-two playing cards (in a square about nine inches by nine inches) in 0.5 minutes.

Figure 4.4 A table of ratings

We can now consider an example, using the formula shown at Figure 4.3:

$$\text{selected basic time} = \text{selected observed time} \times \frac{\text{observed rating}}{\text{standard rating}}$$

Suppose that a task has been observed (timed) and the effective cycle time established as six minutes. The average rating is observed to be 120 on the

British Standard scale. Therefore the observed worker is working at above average pace. The formula gives

$$\text{selected basic time} = 6 \times \frac{120}{100} \text{ minutes}$$

$$= 7.2 \text{ minutes}$$

Thus the selected basic time allowed for this task is more than the time recorded by the observer. Conversely, if the worker had been observed at a rating below 100, then the time observed would be reduced.

In practice, as each cycle of an element of work is observed, it is simultaneously rated. Individual extensions then take place, to produce individual selected basic times for each of the cycles.

O and M and work study practitioners receive training in rating: the most common method is to test their judgements against a large number of films showing a wide variety of work being performed. Figure 4.5 is a copy of the third film-rating test given to a beginner on a work study

Film scene	Countersinking		Kick-press		Shearing rubber tiles	
	Observed rate	True rate	Observed rate	True rate	Observed rate	True rate
1	60	64	70	70	90	88
2	110	112	110	125	100	115
3	90	109	75	94	110	124
4	70	84	70	84	90	88
5	100	112	100	125	110	103

Figure 4.5   Rating test number three

course. The test consists of being shown five scenes of three tasks undertaken in a working environment: countersinking, operating a kick-press and shearing rubber tiles. Figure 4.6 shows a plot of the fifteen exercises. This is a convenient graphical method of showing students their progress and enables the tutor to gain a quick impression. This particular student is seen to be rather mean with his ratings: for example, in the rubber tile scene, on one occasion he sees a pace of 110 when it is actually much faster, namely 124.

Relaxation allowance. Having arrived at a fair selected basic time, we go on to add the relaxation allowance (RA), which is defined in BS 3138: 1969 as 'an addition to the basic time intended to provide the worker with the opportunity to recover from the physiological and psychological effects of carrying out specified work under specified conditions and to allow attention to personal needs. The amount of allowance will depend on the nature of the job.'

Figure 4.7 gives an idea of the kind of factors taken into consideration

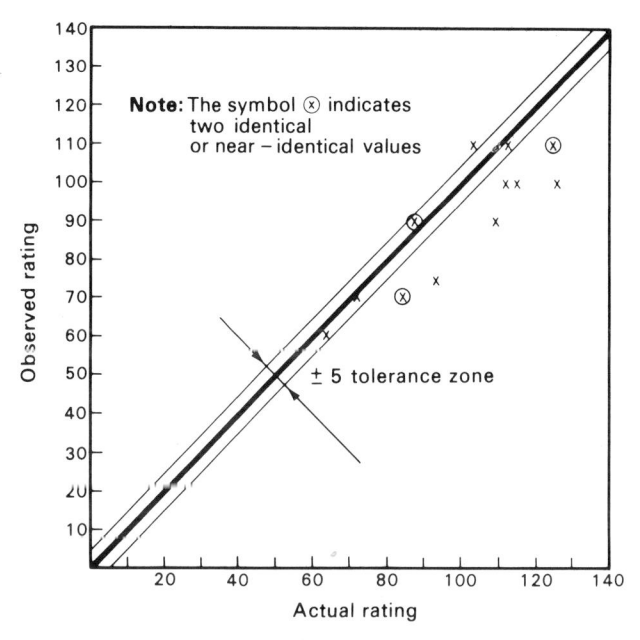

Applied work study principles—the standard time

Figure 4.6 Rating graph: an early attempt at rating by a trainee

when arriving at a fair relaxation allowance, to be added to the selected basic time (see Figure 4.3).

Taking up the example of our basic time of 7.2 minutes, let us suppose that the work is being done by a female in a normal standing position. There is no use of force and the work is fine or exacting; there is no disturbing noise level or mental strain; there is high monotony and the work is very tedious. The total percentage allowance, using the table in Figure 4.7, is arrived at as follows:

personal allowance		7
basic fatigue		4
standing allowance		4
exacting work		2
monotony		4
tediousness		2
	total	23 per cent

Basic work content. It is now possible to calculate the basic work content, as follows:

EXTRACT (percentages to be added to basic time)

		Male	Female
A.	*Constant*		
	Personal	5	7
	Basic fatigue	4	4
B.	*Variable*		
	(i) Standing	2	4
	(ii) Abnormal position		
	Awkward (bending)	2	3
	Very awkward, lying or stretching up	7	7
C.	*Use of Force*		
	Weight lifted (lb)		
	10	1	2
	20	3	4
	40	9	13
	70		22 (max.)
D.	*Close attention*		
	Fine or exacting work	2	2
	Very fine or very exacting	5	5
E.	*Noise level*		
	Intermittent, loud	2	2
	Intermittent, very loud, high pitched, loud	5	5
F.	*Mental strain*		
	Complex or wide span of attention	4	4
	Very complex	8	8
G.	*Monotony*		
	Medium	1	1
	High	4	4
H.	*Tediousness*		
	Tedious	2	1
	Very	5	2

Note: Allowances may also be added for bad light and atmospheric conditions, although every effort should be made, by the practice of ergonomics principles, to remove such adverse factors.

Figure 4.7 Relaxation allowances

selected basic time   7.2 minutes

add $\frac{23}{100} \times 7.2$ 1.7 minutes

basic work content   8.9 minutes   (See Figure 4.3.)

We must now consider two possible further allowances to be added.

Work contingency allowance. This is an addition to the basic work content and caters for legitimate and expected items of work such as the following:

1. Cases where an operator is required to occasionally inspect his own work or process
2. Process rejects: for example, where a piece of work can occasionally jam in a machine
3. Rectification work

Applied work study principles—the standard time

4. Tool adjustments
5. Cases where an operator has to replenish his own stocks: for example, an office print machine operator who has to occasionally visit the store room or receive stocks of paper

If there is a case for a work contingency allowance to be added, this is done and the resulting time is then known as the total work content, which gives the following formula:

basic work content + work contingency allowance = total work content

It is now only necessary to add an allowance for any delays that may exist.

Delay contingency allowance. This is an allowance to cater for legitimate and expected delays, such as machine-dictated delays (the operator has to wait until his machine completes its contribution) or telephone interruptions, where answering the telephone is not part of the person's job specification but he is required to answer the telephone if no one else is there. This can often happen in office work.

If there is a case for a delay contingency allowance to be added, this is done and the resulting time is then known as the standard time, which gives the following formula:

total work content + delay contingency allowance = standard time

It is then usual to talk of a standard minutes or standard hours value.

It does not follow that a company will settle for the standard time. If desired, company policy may wish to make additional allowances, such as policy bonuses and bonus increments. However, the important thing is that the standard time is not tampered with. The standard time forms the basis for planning machine and manpower requirements: the policy allowances only increase cash payment and not work content.

In practice, the standard time is compiled by timing each cycle and rating it individually (unless the cycle time is extremely short, in which case a blanket rating is given for the impression of a number of cycles). The selected basic times are then totalled and the arithmetic mean average calculated, to which are added the allowances already discussed.

Examination questions

1. What is meant by critical examination in method study?
   (NEBSS Certificate, 1970)
2. Describe a work situation in which the application of work study should improve productivity. Outline how the study should be carried out and the benefits which might result.
   (NEBSS Certificate, 1969)
3. Describe how to establish standard times for work done in a general typing pool.
   (IWSP Graduate Examination, 1969)

4. Outline the steps you would take in introducing work study into a working situation where it has not previously been applied.
(City & Guilds *Work Study*, 1969)
5. A standard time is in dispute and you have been asked to investigate. What steps would you take?
(IWSP Graduate Examination, 1969)
6. Describe the principal ways used to record the facts during a method study assignment. Give an example of the use of one of them.
(City & Guilds *Work Study*, 1968)
7. How would you conduct the critical examination stage of a method study assignment?
(City & Guilds *Work Study*, 1968)
8. Define each of the following and comment on their differences:
   (i) allowed times
   (ii) standard times
   (iii) basic times (City & Guilds *Work Study*, 1968)
9. Discuss the following statement, giving both sides of the argument: 'Time study is a curse of modern civilization: it imposes unfair burdens on personnel, encourages poor quality work and is a cause of disputes and bad industrial relations. It should be banned from modern business life.'
10. Explain what is understood by
    (i) critical examination
    (ii) primary questions
    (iii) secondary questions
    (iv) progressive elimination
    Explain why the sequence of the primary and secondary questions is important.
(IWSP *Method Study—Technical and Clerical*, 1974)
11. (i) Explain why it is necessary to have the co-operation of supervision during method study.
    (ii) How could supervisors assist the work study practitioner?
(IWSP *Method Study—Technical and Clerical*, 1974)
12. Discuss the implication of the select stage in relation to the choice of method study projects, in both the technical and clerical fields.
(IWSP *Method Study—Technical and Clerical*, 1972)
13. (i) At what stage in a method study investigation should critical examination take place?
    (ii) Explain why it should take place at this stage.
    (iii) Describe the critical examination procedure in detail.
(IWSP *Method Study—Technical and Clerical*, 1973)
14. (i) What is understood by work measurement?
    (ii) Describe the main uses of the information derived from work measurement.
(IWSP *Work Measurement, Technical and Clerical*, 1974)

15. (i) Why are relaxation allowances necessary?
    (ii) How can they be assessed?
    (iii) Describe six factors that could influence the amount of the relaxation allowance.
    (IWSP *Work Measurement—Technical and Clerical*, 1974)
16. Given the basic minutes per element, describe four adjustments which may be necessary to produce a standard minute value per job. Show clearly how these adjustments are effected.
    (IWSP *Work Measurement—Technical and Clerical*, 1972)
17. Discuss the various allowances that may be added to basic times and why such allowances are made.
    (IWSP *Work Measurement—Technical and Clerical*, 1973)
18. Explain, with reasons, why environmental conditions should be considered during a method study.
    (IWSP *Associated Techniques B*, 1974)
19. Discuss the organization of work to overcome
    (i) fatigue
    (ii) boredom
    (IWSP *Associated Techniques B*, 1974)
20. Discuss the use and importance of work study in industry, mentioning the available techniques and their relationships with types of industries and industrial relations.
    (Institution of Works Managers, college paper)
21. Examine the purposes of work study in production management. How do you account for the comparative neglect of this important tool of management in the past?
    (Institution of Work Managers, college paper)
22. Allowances of various kind are included in time study calculations. What are these allowances, and why are they considered necessary?
    (Institution of Works Managers, college paper)
23. Describe briefly the steps involved in improving the efficiency of an assembly bench operation.
    (Institution of Works Managers, college paper)
24. Objection is sometimes raised to the introduction of an incentive scheme which offers extra pay for extra work, on the grounds that such a scheme would tend to lower the quality of work. What proposals would you make to maintain the quality standard and how would they assist in doing so?
    (Institution of Works Managers, college paper)
25. Describe the basis and method of using the questioning technique in work study.
    (Institution of Works Managers, college paper)
26. Variations in actual times for a specified element may be due to factors outside or within the control of the worker. What outside factors do you consider could create variations, and why?
    (City & Guilds *Work Study*, 1973)

27. (i) Define and explain the term 'policy allowance'.
(ii) Give an example of circumstances in which this allowance would be made.

(City & Guilds *Work Study*, 1973)

28. What steps should be taken before a new method is installed in order to ensure that the change-over is as smooth as possible?

(City & Guilds *Work Study*, 1974)

29. From the times, ratings and percentage relaxation allowances given in Table 4.1, calculate:
(i) the standard time per box of pens packed
(ii) the staff required to pack 2800 gross of boxes per 40 hour week, assuming an average overall performance of 95.

(City & Guilds *Work Study*, 1974)

Element	Representative observed ratings	Representative observed times	% RA	Notes
1. Pick up and position empty box	95	0.05	9	
2. Pack 12 pens in box	85	0.25	11	
3. Close box and secure with two seals	80	0.13	11	
4. Place aside 12 full boxes	105	0.15	11	
5. Obtain supply of empty boxes from store	85	0.76	10	Average no. brought = 95
6. Obtain supply of pens	75	1.98	10	Average no. brought = 1500
7. Replenish seal holders	90	0.36	10	Holder contains 1200 seals
8. Arrange workplace	105	0.35	11	After bringing supply of empty boxes

Table 4.1

5
Statistical aids

5.1 Methods and examples

Some writers refer to statistics as a science which is concerned with the comparison of numbers. Others say that statistics is not a science but a 'scientific method' which may be defined as 'the collection, presentation, analysis and interpretation of numerical data'. Confusion in the public mind about the subject may arise from the fact that statistics has *two* meanings:
1. Statistics are a collection of comparable figures relating to a subject or in a related group: for example, rainfall figures.
2. Statistics is a collection of methods of treating or processing a series of figures.

The second meaning can be further divided into descriptive statistics and inductive statistics.

Descriptive statistics. This term refers to the treatment of data with the aim of describing characteristics. For example, the arithmetic mean of the following five numbers (10, 9, 11, 8, 12) taken from a larger group is 10 (i.e. 50 divided by 5). This is a descriptive statistic which represents the group in a particular way.

Inductive statistics. These are concerned with making forecasts, estimates and judgements relating to a larger group of data than the group actually available to the analyst. In the case of the arithmetic mean mentioned, if the mean calculated is used to predict the mean of the larger group of data from which it is drawn, it is an inductive statistic. The basis of inductive statistics is the theory of probability.

Both descriptive and inductive statistics are used in management and applications include the following:
1. The theory of probability applied to activity sampling
2. The analysis of machine performance
3. Sampling techniques used in quality control inspection
4. Work study calculations
5. General descriptive statistics used in comparing performances such as the comparison of wages paid to groups of workers

Standard deviation. Unfortunately, a statistic such as the arithmetic mean does not give a measure of the dispersion of the values about itself, and such a measure would provide useful information on the variability of performance within the group. A statistic which can provide useful information on this aspect is known as the standard deviation (or root mean square deviation). It may be calculated as follows:
1. Measure the deviation (or difference) of each reading from the arithmetic mean.
2. Square each deviation and calculate the arithmetic mean of the sum of these squares.
3. Find the square root of this mean.

We can illustrate this procedure by taking again our example of five numbers (10, 9, 11, 8, 12), the sum of which is 50. The arithmetic mean is

$$\frac{50}{5} = 10$$

The deviations are 0, 1, 1, 2, 2 and the squares of the deviations are 0, 1, 1, 4, 4. The sum of these is 10 and the mean of these squared number is

$$\frac{10}{5} = 2$$

Thus the standard deviation = the square root of 2.

The following formula provides an easier method of calculation, since it avoids having to calculate the individual deviations:

$$\text{standard deviation (SD) of } n \text{ numbers} = \frac{\text{the sum of the squares of the numbers} - \frac{\text{the sum of the numbers all squared and then divided by } n}{\text{all divided by } n}}$$

Thus from our example:

$$SD = \text{square root of } \frac{510 - \frac{2500}{5}}{5} = \text{square root of 2, as before.}$$

The standard deviation is an immensely important statistic, particularly in inductive statistics connected with sampling techniques of various kinds. In work measurement, for example, two groups of selected basic times can be compared using their standard deviations to measure the degree of 'settling' of times around a mean.

Because the standard deviation is a square root, it is stated mathematically as plus or minus. Thus in the above example, the standard deviation is plus or minus the square root of two, which is plus or minus 1.414. Remember that this is a measure of dispersion or spread about the arithmetic mean.

Statistical aids

Averages. Although people often talk of average scores or average wages, there are different kinds of averages, the arithmetic mean being only one of them. The following work study examination question is of relevance here.

The following data was obtained during a time study of the same process:

Number of occurrences	Basic minutes
1	1.85
3	2.60
2	1.75
10	2.92
1	1.80
1	1.55
5	2.80
2	1.40

Explain each of the following terms and calculate them for the data given:
  (i) *the weighted average*
  (ii) *the mode*
  (iii) *the simple arithmetic average*
  (v) *the median*
Which would you use to calculate a standard time and why?

Answer (i)—the weighted average takes into account the frequency with which each time occurs, and it is calculated as follows:

```
 1 × 1.85 =  1.85
 3 × 2.60 =  7.80
 2 × 1.75 =  3.50
10 × 2.92 = 29.20
 1 × 1.80 =  1.80
 1 × 1.55 =  1.55
 5 × 2.80 = 14.00
 2 × 1.40 =  2.80
 ──          ─────
 25          62.50
```
weighted average 2.50 minutes

Answer (ii)—the mode (or modal average) is simply the most frequently occurring time. Thus mode = 2.92 minutes.

Answer (iii)—the simple arithmetic average is obtained by adding the basic minutes quoted in the original table and dividing by the number listed (eight in this case).

Thus the simple arithmetic average $= \dfrac{16.67}{8}$

= 2.08 minutes (approx.)

Answer (iv)—the median is obtained by arranging all the times in ascending order and noting the middle time. If this is done, we have

median time = 2.80 minutes (by inspection).

Before we try to decide on the best (fairest) time, there are two assumptions to state: we assume that the wide variations are due to unavoidable process fluctuations and that no further readings are allowed to us or available.

Figure 5.1 summarizes the four average values and links them with important information concerning the number of values falling above and below the chosen average. It can be seen, for example, that if the

Type of average value chosen	Value (minutes)	Number of values which fall above this chosen average (from 25)	Number of values which fall below this chosen average (from 25)
Weighted	2.50	18	7
Modal	2.92	0	15
Simple arithmetic	2.08	18	7
Median	2.80	10	10

Figure 5.1 Important information concerning the four types of averages calculated from the time study

weighted average is chosen (2.50 minutes), eighteen of the twenty-five times will be larger than this and a shop steward could argue that this was grossly unfair. The situation is certainly an unusual one, but variations in the basic time could be due to fluctuations in power supply and the constitution of materials used, inconsistent operator(s) or fluctuations in process steam or water supply.

Very keen readers may wish to calculate the standard deviation of these twenty five readings:

standard deviation = 0.55 (approx.)

Skewed distribution. The same readers may also wish to plot a frequency distribution chart (vertical axis representing number of times a particular reading occurs, the horizontal axis representing the actual times). The resulting curve is interesting but rather odd. If a curve is pushed over towards left or right, it is said to be skewed: see Figure 5.2. A coefficient of skewness can be calculated, as follows:

$$\text{coefficient of skewness} = \frac{3\,(\text{arithmetic mean} - \text{median})}{\text{standard deviation}}$$

$$= \frac{3 \times (2.50 - 2.80)}{0.55}$$

$$= -\frac{0.90}{0.55}$$

$$= -1.63 \text{ (approx.)}$$

Statistical aids

A highly skewed distribution may have a value of plus or minus one and values up to plus or minus three are theoretically possible. The negative sign indicates the tail of the distribution is skewed (pushed) to the left and skewed to the smaller values of the basic minutes.

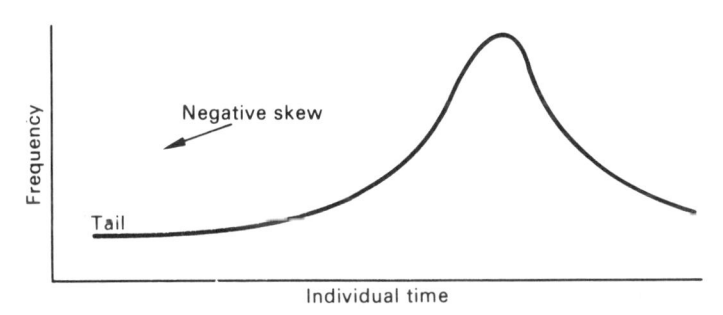

Figure 5.2 A negative (left) skew

We may suggest a summary on our examination as follows:
1. The weighted arithmetic mean gives a mathematically true average which includes all the readings.
2. Insufficient readings have been taken to justify a statistically accurate standard being set, bearing in mind the wide range of readings (1.40 to 2.92 minutes). We shall see in a later part of this chapter that at least seventy readings are required.
3. Further readings, if taken, would suggest a tendency in favour of the high readings, 2.80 and 2.92 (fifteen out of twenty-five), by the laws of probability.
4. The coefficient of skewness (−1.63) indicates the tail of the distribution is to the left and the distribution is skewed to the smaller values.
5. In the absence of any further readings, the median value (2.80 minutes) could be the best compromise, if a decision must be made. It would probably offer the best basis for negotiating a temporary-time with the shop floor, on the understanding that a modified time could be issued in the light of more readings becoming available.

This example will serve to indicate to supervisors that there is more to establishing a fair time for a piece of work than might seem apparent at first.

Number of readings. Variations in time for individual cycles in normal situations may result from such influences as differences in the exact position of the parts and tools used; variations in reading the stop watch; difficulties in deciding on the exact end-point at which the watch reading is made; subjective judgement of operator movements and pace. Since work measurement is a process of sampling, the greater the number of cycles timed the better: the result will thus be a closer representation of the activity under observation.

Naturally, the expense of a study is in direct proportion to the number of cycles timed and we need to know the minimum readings required, in order to achieve a known accuracy. Statisticians have devised formulae for this purpose, one of which is

$$R = \left[\frac{40\sqrt{NA-B}}{C} \right]^2$$

where

R = number of readings necessary to predict the true time with 95 per cent certainty and a tolerance of plus or minus 5 per cent
N = number of readings already taken in study
A = sum of all the squares of the individual readings
B = square of the sum of all the individual readings
C = sum of all the individual readings
NA = N times A

If we apply this formula to the examination question previously discussed we can proceed as follows:

N = 25 (readings)
A = 164 (approx.)
B = $(62.5)^2$
C = 62.5

and we can substitute into the formula:

$$N = \left[\frac{40\sqrt{25 \times 164 - (62.5)^2}}{62.5} \right]^2$$

$$= \left[\frac{40\sqrt{180}}{62.5} \right]^2$$

= 74 readings required (plus or minus 5 per cent)

This means that we can be certain, 95 times out of 100, that we should take between 70 and 78 readings. Thus, to be statistically safe, we should take a further (78−25) readings, namely 53 readings. Readers may now care to try an exercise.

Thirty observations are taken of a repetitive clerical operation, and the following selected basic times are obtained:

Time (minutes)	Number of times observed
6	14
8	1
5	14
7	1
	30

Have enough readings been taken?

Correlation Coefficients. One of our main objectives in using applied statistics in management is to estimate values of one factor by making reference to values of an associated factor. When relationships between factors are of a quantitative nature, statisticians use a technique known as correlation for identifying and measuring such relationships. Correlation is seen, then, to be concerned with the study of co-relatedness.

Variables are correlated if they behave in such a way that changes in the value of one are associated with changes in the value of the other, so that it is possible to predict the value of one variable, if the value of the other variable is known. Correlation coefficients are a statistical attempt to assign a numerical value to the co-relatedness of two sets of data. They are expressed in a value range between plus one and minus one: the nearer the value is to one of these two extreme values, the closer is the correlation. Generally speaking, if the correlation coefficient is positive, then we have direct correlation and a straight line graph would slope up to the right: for example, when plotting the sales of soft drinks (vertically) against average daytime temperature (horizontally). If the correlation coefficient is negative, then we have inverse correlation and the straight line graph would slope up to the left. This could happen when plotting the sales of pullovers against average day-time temperature.

The Pearsonian coefficient gives us a practical method of measuring correlation. Let us suppose that we plot the vertical (dependent variable) values on a Y axis and the horizontal (independent variable) values on an X axis. Individual values plotted against these axes may then be referred to as y-values and x-values.

As an illustration, we might return to our example of the trainee O and M or work study officer, in the early stages of training in rating (see Figure 4.6, page 53). For simplicity, we shall consider his first ten attempts (in this 15-scene test). Observant students will notice a similarity between this method and that for calculating standard deviation, namely using deviations from the arithmetic mean (x and y respectively). Summations of the squares of these values are then calculated and used in the Pearsonian equation, as follows:

$$P = \frac{\text{sum of } xy}{\sqrt{\text{sum of } x^2 \times \text{sum of } y^2}}$$

Figure 5.3 gives the calculations for arriving at the Pearsonian correlation coefficient (P). Substituting values in the formula:

$$P = \frac{3428}{\sqrt{4319 \times 3125}}$$

$P = +\ 0.94$ (approx.)

This value is quite close to 1.0 and indicates a good degree of correlation between the student's assessments and the actual values from the rating film.

Actual rating X	64	112	109	84	112	70	125	94	84	125	Arithmetic mean (approx.) = 98
Observed rating Y	60	110	90	70	100	70	110	75	70	100	Arithmetic mean (approx.) = 86
Deviations (x) from mean of 98	−34	+14	+11	−14	+14	−28	+27	−4	−14	+27	sum
	1156	196	121	196	196	784	729	16	196	729	squared 4319
Deviations (y) from mean of 86	−26	+24	+4	−16	+14	−16	+24	−11	−16	+14	sum
	676	576	16	256	196	256	576	121	256	196	squared 3125
Product of x multiplied by y	885	336	44	224	196	448	649	44	224	378	Sum of xys 3428

Figure 5.3 Calculation for Pearsonian correlation coefficient

Statistical aids

It should be remembered that the correlation coefficient indicates how close to the straight line (shown in Figure 4.6) the student's readings are when plotted graphically. It does not attempt to measure the slope of the student's line of best fit, drawn through his ten observation values, which is shown in Figure 5.4. The slope is important in work measurement rating, as well as the correlation. The student's line of best fit is seen to

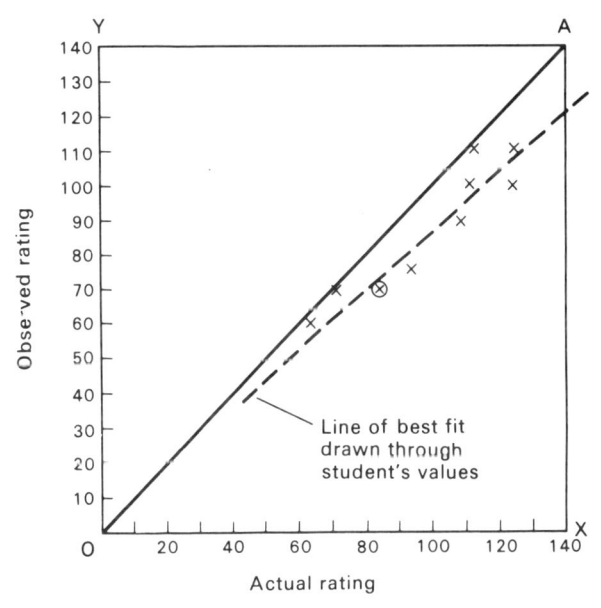

Figure 5.4 Work study trainee's rating test results: ten scenes from rating films 'Countersinking' and 'Kick-press'

fall below the theoretical diagonal OA towards the top end. This indicates a weakness in rating and is known as 'tightness'; to be blunt, the student is being mean and this could lead to trouble with shop floor operatives if the error is allowed to go uncorrected.

It is sometimes useful to arrange two sets of values in order of importance (ranking) and then to measure one ranking against the other, using a *rank correlation coefficient*. One such coefficient is the Spearman coefficient(s), as follows:

$$S = 1 - \frac{6 \times (\text{sum of differences})^2}{(N^2 - 1) \times N}$$

where 'differences' = the difference between one person's ranking and another person's, for example
N = number of items in the ranking

Let us consider an example. Seven supervisors are competing for the post of assistant works manager. They are given a written management test and are also ranked by a management committee on job performance. The results are shown in Table 5.1.

Supervisor	Ranking on written test	Ranking by management committee	Difference	Difference squared
Jones	7	6	1	1
Smith	4	3	1	1
Watkins	1	2	1	1
Friar	5	5	0	0
Walsh	2	1	1	1
Greenwood	6	7	1	1
Roberts	3	4	1	1
			TOTAL:	6

Table 5.1

$$\text{Spearman rank correlation coefficient} = 1 - \frac{6 \times 6}{7(49-1)}$$

$$= 1 - \frac{36}{336}$$

$$= +0.89 \text{ (approx.)}$$

This indicates a strong correlation (nearly 0.9) between the written test and the opinions of the management team. The suggestion is that the written test is a useful one and could economize on management time: it might also be useful when recruiting supervisors from outside the organization.

Another useful example of the use of the rank correlation coefficient is in the examination of pay structures. The study of one small company's pay structure revealed twenty categories of labour, with wage payment ranging from £0.990 per clock hour (gross pay) to £0.318. The arithmetic mean average pay rate was £0.672 with a range of the same amount. These categories were ranked in size order and alongside they were then ranked from the viewpoint of bonus as a percentage of gross pay. A rank correlation coefficient was computed, +0.77, and it was thus seen that a reasonable degree of correlation existed. The higher the gross pay per clock-hour, the higher was the percentage which the bonus element occupied in the whole pay. This was a reasonable indication that the personnel concerned were responding favourably to the idea of incentive payment.

Activity sampling. This is 'a technique in which a large number of observations are made over a period of time of one or a group of machines, processes or workers. Each observation records what is happening at that instant and the percentage of observations recorded for

Statistical aids

a particular activity or delay is a measure of the percentage of time during which that activity or delay occurs.' (British Standard 3138: 1969.) It is known by other names, such as ratio-delay study, observation ratio study, snap-reading method, random observation method, work sampling and performance sampling. However, whatever the name or variation of individual technique, the object of activity sampling is always the same. It is to obtain as accurate a record as possible of what is happening in a work situation, for the minimum cost in observer's time.

Activity sampling is one of the most powerful techniques in the work study repertoire and will be very useful for any supervisor undertaking project report work for such examining bodies as the National Examinations Board in Supervisory Studies (NEBSS), the Institution of Works Managers (IWM) and the Institute of Work Study Practitioners (IWSP). It is first thought to have been used as a technique of work measurement in 1927. The man responsible, L. H. C. Tippett, was a research worker in the British cotton industry. Tippett's interest was in the productivity of looms, bearing in mind such factors as broken warp threads and machine faults. He developed a method of taking instant readings of groups of machines and workers in order to measure such aspects as machine downtime and its reasons, the proportions of working-to-idle ratios and to take a general look at various workplace activities.

Naturally, the most accurate method of recording the activities in a workplace situation is to stay there all the time and continually record the events taking place. In practice, we do not need absolute accuracy in such work any more than an engineering designer needs it. For example, a designer may complete some complex calculations for a steel shaft diameter, finding it to be $4\frac{5}{32}$ inches. The shaft must run in roller bearings and it may be more convenient to buy and fit the next larger (standard) size of bearing, having a bore size of $4\frac{1}{4}$ inches. The concentration on dimensional accuracy must be confined to the machining of the shaft diameters so as to ensure the correct running fits. Activity sampling enables us to plan carefully the frequency and number of observations to make and enables a sufficiently accurate interpretation to be drawn from the analysis.

We can summarize the advantages of activity sampling over continuous sampling as follows:

1. As already mentioned, it is much more economical in observer's time. The cost of an activity sampling study may be only around one-fifth of the cost of a continuous sampling study.
2. Activity sampling studies can be undertaken, in many cases, by relatively unskilled observers, providing that they work under the guidance of a work study or O and M practitioners.
3. Activity sampling very conveniently allows the whole operations of a department or area to be studied and recorded over the same

general time period. This can be a big advantage, for example, when studying the movements of people and paperwork between a number of offices in a building.

4. Since the whole subject of directly observing people at work is hedged with practical and psychological problems of disturbance, activity sampling is to be preferred through being not nearly so disturbing as continuous sampling. In fact, during activity sampling the observer may not be noticed at all.

Readers should note that neither activity sampling nor continuous sampling can accurately measure work that contains a large proportion of mental work. However, it is quite suitable for most repetitive manual and clerical activities.

Activity sampling can be put to many uses, including supplying the answers to the following questions:

1. Is the recorded proportion of idle time acceptable in the particular situation? Should it be reduced by re-allocation of duties or by the reduction or elimination of interruptions?
2. Is the distribution of effort reasonable?
3. Are the results achieved a reasonable return on the effort expended on the various activities? Comparative results for different sections employed on similar work will be available and yield useful information in this respect.
4. How are the personnel measuring up to some previously set yardstick of performance (that may not be directly measurable in terms of a product made)?
5. Do the office or workshop equipment and machinery justify retention?
6. Is the potential use of equipment and machinery likely to be worthwhile in terms of the possible saving of time?
7. Are there clear indications of activities and areas likely to yield benefits from further investigation or full work study or O and M investigations?

It should be made clear at this point that the method of sampling chosen will be dependent on the particular problem situation. Thus an O and M officer may decide to use a combination of activity sampling and continuous sampling, or fixed-interval sampling during continual presence, depending on the individual circumstances. Summarizing these as definite points in order to avoid confusion, we have the following methods of approach:

1. The use of conventional activity sampling, which depends on random visits to the workshop or office area and instant readings taken at those times.
2. Continuous sampling in an area: for example, in a busy office it may be decided to record all telephone activity in the office. An observer would stay in the office and do this, breaking the traffic down into

Statistical aids

incoming and outgoing calls, internal telephones and external telephones.
3. Fixed-interval, continual presence sampling. This could take the form of an observer staying in an office and taking a number of instantaneous readings every three minutes of all the activities: these might be divided into telephone activity, callers to the office and activities of personnel.
4. Full-scale O and M investigations are often preceded by pilot studies, using activity sampling (readings on a random basis). The object is to discover areas likely to yield profitable results for the expensive study planned.

The following notes, taken from the training programme of an O and M department, may help to give the reader a clearer picture of the general approach to sampling methods in office areas.

'CLERICAL ACTIVITY SAMPLING METHOD: Readings should be chosen so as to give as representative a spread as possible. A minimum period would probably be three weeks and if possible two of these periods in the year for comparison.

Because of the variety of duties performed in the office, it is important to have time during the study to ask an officer what he or she is doing (this is not as obvious in clerical observations as it is, for example, in a workshop). A clerical worker may have 20 or more duties.

If readings are taken at very frequent intervals, then apart from the possibility of losing an accurate overall picture of the situation, one may be misled by the application of activity sampling formulae as to the number of readings required. A frequency of the order of 3 minutes is probably most suitable for continuous sampling, but this will be governed by the numbers of staff being observed and the number of observers. A record should be made of other large duties which are undertaken outside the study period: these may be averaged out over the year and the sampling figures amended.

Extreme care should be taken when applying the "*not-working*" category. It is often a very small category for office applications and can be merged into "miscellaneous". However, this may be quite the opposite for studies of manual operations. A road-digging job may feature one man virtually watching the other all the time. Such studies will generally yield only a few categories of activity: these will repeat continually and activity sampling over one or two days will probably yield accurate figures.

It is important to decide what constitutes "not working" for an office worker. If we consider a ledger clerk, for example, it would be unwise to regard any of his time at the desk when he was not actually putting pen to paper as "not working". In a case where the clerk is holding his pen but looking straight ahead or at some paperwork, he might even be credited as "working", using the reverse of the method. However, if he is sitting back and smoking, or talking with a colleague about an event of the previous evening, these are obviously "not-working" categories.

If the observer feels (from his experience of office work) that there is not sufficient application to the work, and the duty in question is a substantial portion of the clerk's duties, then a method study and time study may be carried out on that duty. It will then be necessary to ascertain how much thinking and calculating time elapses before an entry is made in the ledger. The observer may have to make specimen calculations himself.

The experienced work study observer will look principally for new methods of work in the clerical sphere. The most useful results of activity sampling are a list of all the duties carried out in the office(s) in question and an approximation of the amount of time spent on each duty.'

Activity sampling observation-recording form									Using random readings table:
Date of study	8th May 75	Observer	\multicolumn{5}{c	}{J. Smeeton O and M Dept.}		No. 16
Department and section studied	\multicolumn{2}{c	}{Purchasing department order-raising section}	\multicolumn{2}{c	}{Day of study}	\multicolumn{3}{c	}{(Wednesday)}		First reading at ....
Activity	\multicolumn{8}{c	}{Time of study period}	
	9.0 / 10.0	10.0 / 11.0	11.0 / 12.0	12.0 / 1.0	1.0 / 2.0	2.0 / 3.0	3.0 / 4.0	4.0 / 5.0	Total readings
	\multicolumn{8}{c	}{Number of readings taken each period}	
Typing orders Miss Jones	⊬⊬⊬ I	⊬⊬⊬ II	III	IIII		IIII	⊬⊬⊬	⊬⊬⊬ I	(35)
Typing orders Mrs Smith	⊬⊬⊬ I	⊬⊬⊬	⊬⊬⊬	⊬⊬⊬ I					(22)
Typing hourly totals	12	12	8	10	Lunch break	4	5	6	(57)

Figure 5.5 Activity sampling observation recording form

The activity sampling observer must take *instantaneous readings*, whether he suddenly appears on the scene or suddenly looks up during a fixed-interval sampling (continual presence) duty. Instantaneous means that the observer should not attempt to guess what the worker has just been doing or might just be going to do: he should simply record the instantaneous event, whether it be working, talking or absent.

As an activity is observed, a stroke should be made in a space adjacent to that activity on the activity sampling study form. When the activity has been observed five times, the fifth time is recorded by making a 'five-bar gate', like this 𝍸, which makes the subsequent counting much easier. Figure 5.5 gives an idea of a recording form.

At the commencement of an investigation, of course, the practitioner has no idea of the range of activities likely to be seen. It is a good idea, therefore, to start a major study by interviewing the personnel involved. The list of duties so obtained can then be entered on the activity sampling form, with spaces left for any unexpected activities, as they are observed during the actual study.

Figure 5.6 gives a suggested layout for an activity sampling weekly analysis sheet. This form groups together the recordings taken on each day in the week. Important information recorded on it includes the total number of readings taken and the designed-accuracy of the results.

Activity sampling analysis sheet

O and M dept.

Dept. ____________ Degree of certainty__________ %

Name____________ Date__________

Total readings__________

Duties or activities	Mon.	Tues.	Wed.	Thurs.	Fri.	Total	%	Accy ± %

Figure 5.6 Activity sampling weekly analysis sheet

Mention should also be made here of the personal activity sampling record sheet (see Figure 5.7) which is useful for issuing to a senior officer, manager or supervisor. They simply carry it about with them and record their activities at the precise times listed. (A manager's secretary can do this whilst he is in the office.) This type of form was used, for example, by a chief ambulance officer in local government: his duties took him outside

Day _____   Date _____

Sampling table : 6

Time	Activity	Time	Activity
8.00 a.m.		2.34 p.m.	
8.30		3.04	
8.35		3.25	
9.09		3.38	
9.39		3.55	
9.53		4.24	
10.17		4.40	
10.41		5.10	
10.58		5.15	
11.08		5.49	
11.22		6.19	
11.28		6.33	
12.06 p.m.		6.57	
12.49		7.21	
12.59		7.38	
1.18		7.48	
2.02		8.02	
2.23		8.08	

Figure 5.7 Personal activity sampling record sheet

Statistical aids 75

the ambulance station, to such places as the town hall, health offices and hospitals.

The three main statistical requirements in *sampling theory*, as far as we are concerned here, are:

1. The degree of confidence required in the results
2. The accuracy (tolerance) permissible in the results (we shall use the symbol $\pm L$ for this)
3. The number of readings taken or required (we shall use the symbol N for this)

Figure 5.8 shows, in tabular form, six formulae that should suffice for all activity sampling work in the present context. It will be useful to take a closer look at the example shown in this figure. An observer has taken

Degrees of confidence	Degree of confidence (per cent)	Number of readings required (N)	Accuracy tolerance ($\pm L$)
1	00.27	$\dfrac{p(100-p)}{L^2}$	$\sqrt{\dfrac{p(100-p)}{N}}$
2	95.45	$\dfrac{4p(100-p)}{L^2}$	$2\sqrt{\dfrac{p(100-p)}{N}}$
3	99.73	$\dfrac{9p(100-p)}{L^2}$	$3\sqrt{\dfrac{p(100-p)}{N}}$

Note: $p=$ the percentage that the activity under consideration represents of the total number of readings. For example, a total of 1000 readings are taken and activity A takes up 200 of these. Its percentage of the whole is

$$\frac{200}{1000} \times 100 = 20 \text{ per cent.}$$

Therefore $p=20$ in our formulae, above.

Figure 5.8 Formulae used in activity sampling theory

1000 readings at random and one of the department's activities (A) takes up 200 of these readings. Activity A's percentage of the whole number of observations is thus

$$\frac{200}{1000} \times 100 = 20 \text{ per cent.}$$

In work study and O and M work-sampling, it is usually accurate enough to adopt the 95.45 per cent confidence level (sometimes known as two degrees of confidence). This means that we can be certain of our answer, within the stated accuracy tolerance (L), 9545 times out of 10 000. This is really very close and the actual results will probably be even closer.

We now need to know how accurate a representation of the true situation this twenty per cent figure is. Using the second formula (Figure 5.8) against two degrees of confidence, we have

$$L = 2\sqrt{\frac{p(100-p)}{N}}$$

$$= 2\sqrt{\frac{20 \times 80}{1000}}$$

$$= 2\sqrt{1.6}$$

$$= \pm 2.53 \text{ (approx.)}$$

Thus, the activity that we are interested in, can be said to occupy 20 per cent, plus or minus 2.53, with 9545 out of 10 000 confidence level. Its percentage of the true situation can therefore be predicted as between 17.47 per cent and 22.53 per cent.

Now let us suppose that we are not satisfied with an accuracy tolerance of plus or minus 2.53 per cent. Suppose we want plus or minus one per cent: how many readings would be required? Using the first formula, against two degrees of confidence again, we have

$$N = \frac{4p(100-p)}{L^2}$$

which substitutes as

$$N = \frac{4 \times 20(100-20)}{1 \times 1}$$

$$= \frac{80 \times 80}{1}$$

$$= 6400 \text{ (readings)}$$

Thus, a further 5400 readings could be required, emphasizing the higher cost of increased accuracy.

In practice, tables can be used to calculate the accuracy tolerance (L) and Figure 5.9 is an example. Readers may wish to trace the above example through it.

A *random sample* is sometimes referred to as a properly drawn sample, or a sample drawn by a random method. It is the method of drawing a sample, not the sample itself, which is random (or unbiased).

Random numbers are required for the unbiased construction of a table of sampling times. By using them we can avoid people's subconscious preferences for a certain number, numbers or number-combinations and also prevent the readings falling on regular but not substantially representative activities, such as tours of inspection and tea breaks.

Tables of randomly generated numbers have been prepared and printed, and these can be used to make up tables to suit any activity

Statistical aids

Per cent of total time occupied by activity or delay	Number of observations				
	10 000	5000	1000	500	100
1	±0.20	±0.28	±0.63	±0.89	±1.99
3	0.34	0.48	1.08	1.52	3.41
5	0.44	0.62	1.38	1.95	4.36
7	0.51	0.72	1.61	2.28	5.10
10	0.60	0.85	1.89	2.68	6.00
15	0.71	1.00	2.26	3.19	7.14
20	**0.80**	**1.13**	**2.53**	**3.58**	**8.00**
25	0.86	1.22	2.74	3.87	8.66
30	0.91	1.29	2.89	4.10	9.17
35	0.95	1.34	3.02	4.27	9.54
40	0.97	1.37	3.09	4.38	9.80
45	0.99	1.39	3.13	4.43	9.91
50	1.00	1.41	3.16	4.47	10.00

Note: The above values may be plotted in graphical form and intermediate values obtained by interpolation.

Figure 5.9 Table for determining the accuracy tolerance (L) for a given number of observations and value of 95 per cent confidence level

sampling investigation. Such a table consists of groups of digits, arranged for easy reference. For example, one table has the following grouping:

1 0 5 5 3 5   2 5 2 4 2 8

Suppose that we need a series of ten three-figure numbers: these can be drawn from the above twelve digits by cycling through from left to right, as follows:

105 055 553 535 352
525 252 524 242 428

Let us now suppose that we wish to design a self-sampling form for a senior officer or manager. It is obvious that he will be too busy to book readings down every minute or two, so we must first decide on a reasonable frequency, say between ten minutes and thirty minutes.

A batch of 118 two-digit numbers are examined in a table of random numbers, and all those between ten and thirty are accepted. These are as follows (and are taken to be elapsed minutes):

Minutes	Minutes	Minutes
29	26	19
18	11	28
19	13	15
27	24	19
24	26	22
20	30	21
23	29	17
18	14	

If the senior officer's day starts at 8.30 a.m. and he has a set lunch break of 12.30–1.30 and finishes at 5 p.m., we could devise observation-times as follows:

Reading			
1	8.59 a.m. (8.30 + 29 minutes)	12	1.42
2	9.17	13	2.08
3	9.36	14	2.38
4	10.03	15	3.07
5	10.27	16	3.21
6	10.47	17	3.40
7	11.10	18	4.08
8	11.28	19	4.23
9	11.54 a.m.	20	4.42
10	12.05 p.m.	21	5.04
11	12.18	22	5.25
			5.42 p.m. (excluded)

We therefore have twenty-two times in the day at which the officer should record his activity at that moment. The time between recordings varies from eleven minutes to thirty minutes.

A different table of reading times can be devised in this way from the random number tables for each of the five working days in the week. If a second week is required to be studied, the devised tables can be cycled around: for example, the table for Monday is used in one week, for Tuesday in the second week, and so on. (See Figure 5.7 for an example of a similar table.)

As an exercise, suppose that a senior officer agrees to use self-sampling over a three-week period. The number of readings taken is thus
$22 \times 15 = 330$
One of the activities is 'In meetings' and 99 readings record this category of activity.
  (i) *Calculate the apparent percentage of his total time spent in meetings.*
  (ii) *If an accuracy of plus or minus five per cent is required in the answer, do we need any more readings? If so, how many (at two degrees of confidence)?*

Careful planning is required if adequate and fair coverage is to be achieved in office sampling, particularly where several offices are being sampled in an overall study. An example of such a case is shown at Figure 5.10, where the O and M department was sampling activity in three offices. The sampling took place over a period of three weeks and it can be seen from the figure that each day in the week was given approximately the same sampling coverage in hours and also over the three different sections of general office, typists' office and clerks' office.

As a last example for students in this chapter, we will set a problem in invoice sampling. Figure 5.11 shows the result of the O and M officer sampling a year's

Statistical aids

	Coverage (hours)			Totals for 3 offices for each day (hours)
	General office	Typists' office	Clerks' office	
Monday	4	6	5	15
Tuesday	4	5	4	13
Wednesday	5	5	4	14
Thursday	4	5	$3\frac{1}{4}$	$12\frac{1}{4}$
Friday	6	$4\frac{1}{2}$	$4\frac{1}{2}$	15
Totals (per week) in hours	23	$25\frac{1}{2}$	$21\frac{1}{4}$	

Figure 5.10 Grouping of activity sampling study hours at the administrative headquarters of a local government department

supply of 10 000 invoices in a supplies department. 972 invoices were selected from the file using random sampling and checked. Ten invoice-value ranges are shown. It is seen that almost 89 per cent of invoices lie in the range £0 to £5.99. This is shown graphically in Figure 5.12.

1. Calculate the accuracy of this estimate with 95.45 per cent certainty (two degrees of confidence).
2. How many invoices would need to be inspected if an accuracy of plus or minus one per cent was necessary?
3. The total value of a year's invoices is £38 000 and the errors detected by the checking clerks in the 972 invoices inspected amounted to only £25. Can you suggest any plan for reducing the amount of time spent on invoice-checking? The average time for checking one invoice is 15 minutes and the total salary cost of an invoicing clerk is £2000 per annum. (The present procedure is for all invoices to be checked.)

Invoice value range	Total readings	Percentage
1. (less than 50p)	168	17.3
2. (50p to 99p)	155	16.0
3. (£1 to £2.99)	373	38.4
4. (£3 to £5.99)	166	17.1
5. (£6 to £8.99)	32	3.3
6. (£9 to £11.99)	17	1.8
7. (£12 to £14.99)	11	1.1
8. (£15 to £20.99)	19	2.0
9. (£21 to £30.99)	9	1.0
10. (£31 and over)	22	2.0
	972	100.0

Figure 5.11 Percentage distribution of invoices

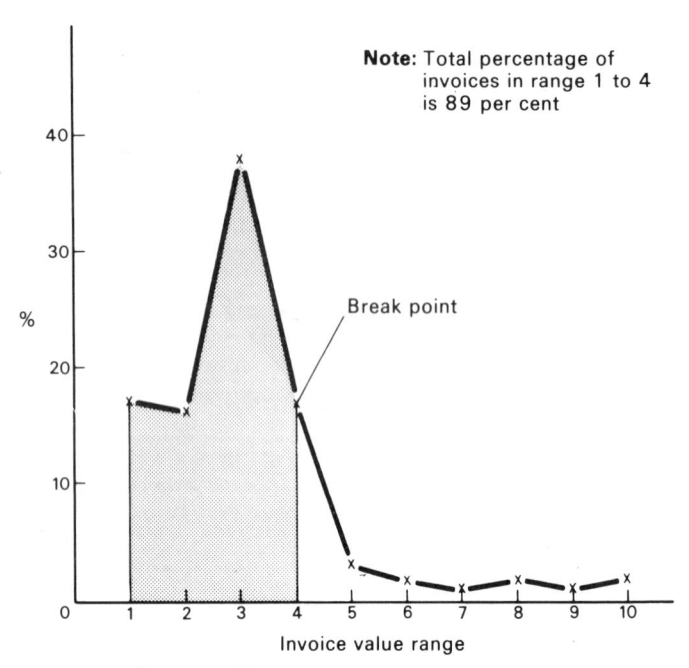

Figure 5.12 Percentage distribution of invoices

Note: Total percentage of invoices in range 1 to 4 is 89 per cent

Examination questions

1. Give one example of a work situation where activity sampling could be usefully applied.

   (NEBSS Certificate, 1968)

2. During a quarter the number of hours lost through breakdown on 12 identical machines was as follows:

Machine No.	Hours Lost
1	100
2	30
3	50
4	70
5	60
6	20
7	50
8	10
9	120
10	30
11	80
12	50

Statistical aids

From this data calculate
   (i) the arithmetic mean
   (ii) the median
   (iii) the mode
Describe the extent to which each of these three statistics can help in analysis of the performance of these machines.
(IWM *Statistics*)

3. (i) Describe the technique of activity sampling.
   (ii) What are the benefits in using activity sampling techniques in carrying out method study investigations?
(IWSP *Method Study—Technical and Clerical*, 1972)

4. (i) In activity sampling what is meant by 'accuracy of results'?
   (ii) Why is it necessary to specify the accuracy required?
   (iii) State, giving reasons, whether or not it is possible to obtain complete accuracy of results by using activity sampling.
(IWSP *Work Measurement—Technical and Clerical*, 1973)

5. Activity sampling is now used to study many types of work.
   (i) In what circumstances would you use it?
   (ii) What observations would you need to record and how would you plan to obtain and record them?
   (iii) How would you assess the number of observations to be recorded?
(City & Guilds *Work Study*, 1973)

6. Explain how activity sampling can be of value in method study investigations.
(City & Guilds *Work Study*, 1974)

6
Applied work study principles—uses of work measurement, specification, payment, planning and cost controls

6.1 The uses of work measurement

We are interested here in the uses of work measurement in O and M work. We are therefore concerned (bearing in mind our earlier definition of O and M) with work measurement in administrative areas of organization, wherever it can be applied, in relation to improving such things as procedures, methods, systems, communications, controls and organization structure. It is nearly always dangerous to generalize in management and the writer would hesitate to exclude work measurement from any of these six areas of O and M activity.

It will be useful at this point for readers to refer back to Chapter 1, where we discussed the financial background to O and M. The financial plan was seen to consist of holding the planned profit in the face of continually increasing costs and often in a competitive market. Market competition may tend to restrict increases in selling price, but the marginal (variable) costs will tend to rise above expected levels due to many factors such as materials price increases, pay awards, increases in power charges and so on. We also discussed in the first chapter the elements of success for a commercial business (and also a local government organization) which were

1. Making a marketable product
2. Maintaining an acceptable quality standard
3. Manufacturing to achieve an acceptable price
4. Ensuring sales

Applied work study principles—uses of work measurement

The overall contribution of O and M falls naturally into three main divisions:
1. The general, organizational view of the whole company operation. For our purposes, work measurement can be excluded from this division.
2. The general methods examination of the company administrative operation, in a search for more economical ways of working. Work measurement is very useful in the basic work study procedure, measuring the present clerical and administrative methods and also new (proposed) methods in an effort to justify the adoption of the better method.
3. Work measurement, in its various forms, over a range of company applications in administrative areas. Typical aims in this case include incentive schemes and the preparation of accurate labour-content estimates for new (hoped for) contracts; these estimates are used in preparing competitive tenders.

In practice, O and M work does not usually cover all aspects of a company operation as expressed in the second and third points above, simply because there is not nearly enough O and M manpower in most companies and organizations to undertake a comprehensive O and M investigation. The areas chosen for the application of work measurement in administration will, therefore, be dictated by individual circumstances. It is hardly surprising, for example, that much of the application of clerical work measurement has taken place in very large companies, which inevitably carry a large fixed overhead cost and a very high break-even ratio. Referring back to the break-even chart (Figure 1.1, page 5), the break-even dimension x should be as small a percentage of the base line AE as possible. A very healthy figure could be 50 per cent but a very large company, carrying enormous research and development (R and D) facilities, may show a percentage in the region of 80 or more per cent. In such companies, every effort must be made to reduce the very high fixed overhead costs.

Figure 6.1 attempts to show the possible (most probable) areas of application for work measurement in O and M work. It is difficult to single out any area from it as being the most important, since different types of organizations have different problems at different times. However, the following list is probably representative of most efforts to use work measurement in O and M:
1. Establishing manpower requirements in administrative areas
2. Setting correct work standards as a basis for performance assessment and financial incentives
3. Ensuring the best use of office space and office machinery
4. Ensuring the most economical use of power, stationery and communications media

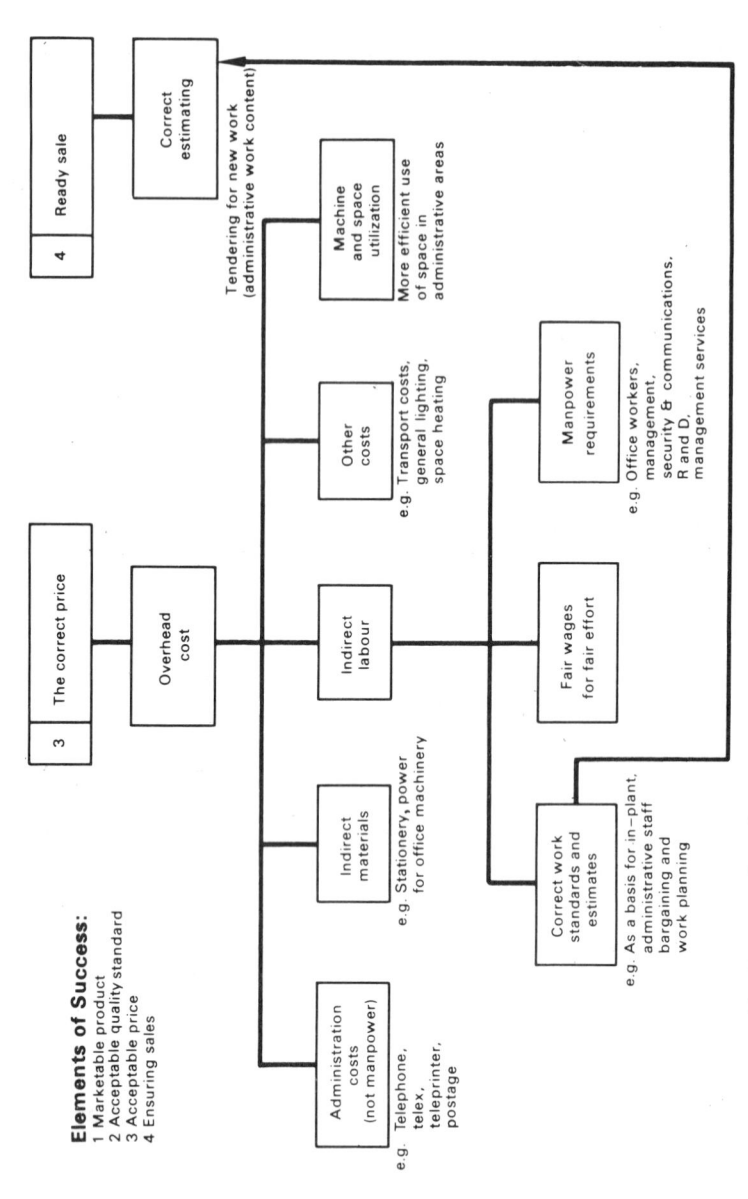

Elements of Success:
1 Marketable product
2 Acceptable quality standard
3 Acceptable price
4 Ensuring sales

Figure 6.1 Possible (most probable) areas of application for work measurement in O and M work

6.2 Work specification

This is 'a document setting out the details of an operation or job, how it is to be performed, the layout of the workplace, particulars of machines, tools and appliances to be used, and the duties and responsibilities of the worker. The standard time or allowed time assigned to the job is normally included.' (British Standard 3138: 1969)

The work specification is a vital, concluding stage to a major O and M investigation, for five main reasons:

1. It provides a historical record of how work is done and under what conditions, at the time of implementing the recorded, agreed methods changes
2. It may provide the basis for negotiations and a contract between management and workers
3. It relates any standard times established to the environmental conditions on which they are based
4. It provides a useful (and precise) monitoring device for the implementation of proposed new methods
5. It provides a means for checking to what extent the established values may be used elsewhere on similar work.

Job particulars. The work specification should record particulars of the job, including such relevant details as:

1. The purpose of the job, including a brief description to distinguish it from other jobs
2. The design and condition of the office machinery and equipment, including the frequency of replacement and overhaul: the office layout. Photographs and drawings should be used, since before-and-after representations are particularly useful.
3. The nature and quantities of required materials and services
4. The types and condition of ancillary equipment used, including the frequency of replacement and overhaul
5. The particular methods employed
6. Any quality specifications for the administrative work
7. The surrounding conditions of work. Particular attention should be paid to the recording of square footage of office space per person, cubic footage of office space per person, and lighting levels.

Method specification. In the case of highly repetitive office work (such as is found in the mail order business), basic-motions analysis may need to be precisely defined. Enough detail should be supplied in the work specification to ensure identification of any changes to existing standard times, so they may be clearly seen as changes of method. Where charts are used, copies should be included in the work specification. This is also an appropriate place in which to include details of any safety regulations and precautions, and good housekeeping standards.

Standard times. Full information must be given in the work specification of standard times and all allowances (including policy allowances). This information is vital for such considerations as production planning, cost control, methods improvement and financial incentive schemes.

Tabular summary. Each major operation should have a summary provided, listing such information as reference number of work specification, brief description of the operation's purpose, standard time, work content and any unoccupied time and interference time (for example, delays imposed by office machinery, machine-cycles or telephone interruptions).

Availability and maintenance. Work specifications should be available for inspection by workers' representatives, but the number of copies held in the company should be strictly controlled. These documents clearly include much confidential information regarding the company's production process and great care should be taken of them: they should be protected from fire, loss and theft by good filing systems and a booking in-and-out procedure.

Below is an outline of the manual prepared by the O and M department of a medium-size engineering company after a detailed and extended study of the company's purchasing department.

BUYING PROCEDURES	NO. OF PAGES
1. Terms of reference	4
2. Principles	4
3. Procedures	5
4. Staffing	1
FORM INSTRUCTIONS	
1. Purchasing order	4
2. Purchasing order master sheet	2
3. Purchasing order (continuation)	2
4. Purchasing order master sheet (continuation)	1
5. Goods inward copy (of purchasing order)	2
6. Purchase authorization	2
7. Goods inward note	6
8. Purchasing order punched progress card	10
Total pages	43

These form instructions are a good example of a work specification instruction. The design of paperwork is of vital importance: an error in paperwork may easily pass detection and the implications may become very serious, especially if the paperwork is part of the input to a computer or other machine system. It is important that new forms are fully understood by those who will be required to use them. O and M practitioners take great pains to describe such new features and use the form instructions as a teaching-aid.

Applied work study principles—uses of work measurement 87

The following is a short extract from item 8, the form instruction for the purchasing order punched progress card (actually taking up ten pages in the Manual)

EXPLANATION OF HEADINGS

1. *Reverse face of card:* this is printed with boxes to record goods inward information.

   '*Ref*': this space (0.3 inches wide) is for recording the part code or drawing number of the item on the front face of the card, so that deliveries of goods may be recorded.

   'Delivery 1' to 'Delivery 6': these six spaces (1.1 inches wide each) enable the purchasing department to record deliveries of goods up to six deliveries and allow for eight items of information to be recorded for each delivery, as described in the next eight headings (which are repeated six times).

The headings for this one form instruction were: function, physical data, explanation of headings (see example above) and procedure, this last being subdivided into clipping, progressing, re-filing and information recording. This should help readers to realize the complications of work specifications, but they are only complicated because administrative work is complicated and vital in function.

6.3 Payment

Payment is naturally close to the roots of work measurement applied to administrative work. Since F. W. Taylor first introduced work measurement, it has been quite generally held that individuals and groups will respond to the inducement of increased monetary payment. This is not a matter of opinion, but a fact, proved by long experience.

Incentives. The subject of incentive payments for administrative workers is a fairly new one in the UK, particularly when we mean to imply work-measured financial incentive schemes. The following basic definitions (taken from British Standard 3138: 1969) will provide a useful introduction to our discussion of payment:

1. Incentive: a procedure designed to encourage a desired response from people
2. Financial incentive: an incentive which provides a financial reward related to the degree of success in achieving a desired objective
   (i) Direct: a financial incentive which provides a financial reward specifically related to the worker's own degree of success in achieving a desired objective
   (ii) Indirect: a financial incentive which provides a financial reward not specifically related to the worker's success in achieving a desired objective, e.g. based on the results of other workers only partially within his control.
3. Payment by results: a financial incentive in which the worker's

earnings are related to the work done and to other factors within the control of the individual or the team or group to which he belongs.
4. Work measured incentive: payment by results based on work measurement data.
5. Piece work: a payment by results scheme where the rewards are based on a constant and specified price per unit or piece produced, regardless of the time taken.
6. Premium bonus scheme: a payment by results scheme where the rewards are based on the time saved which is the difference between the allowed time and the time taken for the task. Payment may or may not be directly proportional to results.
7. Measured day-work scheme: a payment by results scheme where a fixed bonus is paid for achieving any performance at or above a predetermined level.

Measured incentive schemes started with direct incentives (item 2 (i)) and the tendency has been to move towards indirect incentives, emphasizing a team effort (item 2 (ii)). Successful applications of schemes depending on teamwork are still too rare.

It may be strongly argued that, whatever scheme is chosen, its basis should be that of work measurement, as in item 4. Other systems are still popular, such as piecework (item 5) because of its simplicity. If a worker knows, for example, that for each piece he completes, he will receive 10 pence, the situation is crystal-clear: but again, the basis must be one of work measurement.

Premium bonus schemes (item 6) are not very popular with trades unions because of the principle of sharing time savings with management, although to be fair we must not forget that the losses are shared as well. The trades unions may object to workers' pay suffering in order to cover up management inefficiency.

Measured day-work schemes (item 7) are probably the most frequently discussed in the UK today, although such schemes have been widely used in the United States for a considerable time. Again, the emphasis is upon teamwork and co-operation with management, and much is expected from first-line supervisors who need to be well-qualified.

Methods of payment. It is nearly eighty years since F. W. Taylor went to Bethlehem Steel Works and conducted his famous studies, resulting in a work measurement-based bonus scheme. It would therefore be very surprising indeed if a number of different payment schemes had not developed. In fact, these schemes are legion and it would require a full book to describe them in detail. For our purposes, a brief summary will suffice:
1. Time-work or day-work:
    (i) 'Straight' day-work
        (a) Day work
        (b) High wages day work

Applied work study principles—uses of work measurement

　　(ii) Measured day-work
　　　　(a) Graded day work
　　　　(b) Graded level day work
　2. Direct payment by results
　　(i) Piece work
　　　　(a) Straight piece work
　　　　(b) Differential piece work:
　　　　　　(*a*) Taylor system
　　　　　　(*b*) Merrick differential, or multiple piece-rate
　　(ii) Combinations of time and piece work.
　　　　(a) Emerson's efficiency system
　　　　(b) Gantt task and bonus scheme
　　　　(c) Bedaux scheme
　3. Barth scheme
　4. Premium bonus method of payment
　　(i) Halsey
　　(ii) Halsey-Weir
　　(iii) Rowan scheme
　5. Accelerating premium bonus
　6. Collective bonus schemes
　　(i) Priestman's production bonus
　7. Special schemes
　　　(i) Profit sharing and co-partnership
　　　(ii) Multi-factor financial schemes
　　　(iii) Geared incentive schemes, including the stabilized geared scheme.

Space will only allow a few descriptive comments about these methods here, but they should suffice to illustrate the general aims and scope, and to sharpen the reader's appetite to read this subject further:

1. (ii): (a) and (b) are schemes based on work measured standards, where a fixed bonus is paid. Various alternative schemes cater for such factors as periodical step-ups for individuals. They aim to encourage teamwork and put more responsibility on supervisors.
2. (i)(b)(*a*): Taylor—day wages not guaranteed, 2 piecework rates fixed.
2. (ii) (a): Emerson—encourages slower worker to do a little better.
2. (ii) (b): Gantt—combination of day wages and a high piece-rate, day wages guaranteed, bonus for foreman.
2. (ii) (c): Bedeaux—time wages paid until 100 per cent efficiency reached.
3: Barth—particularly suitable for apprentices or beginners.
4: Premium bonus gains and losses shared by employer and employee.
5: The bonus to be paid increases at a faster and faster rate. There is inducement for supervisors.
6: Priestman's—group standard and group rewards.
7. (i): Profit sharing—bonus of a percentage or annual earnings. Co-

partnership extension allows bonus to be left with company as shares.

7. (ii): Multi-factor—based on such aspects as work quality, machine utilization, percentage rejects. These factors may be assigned different weightings.

7. (iii): Geared scheme—a payment by results scheme where the rate of change of bonus is constant and the bonus follows a straight line which, if extended below the bonus-starting performance, would not give zero pay at zero performance.

Stabilized geared scheme—a form of geared scheme suitable for maintenance work, for example, or work that is generally difficult to measure accurately. It protects against excessive bonus fluctuations.

It can be seen that there is a wide range of schemes to choose from. It should therefore be possible to devise a suitable scheme for any administrative-area situation, whether it be a typing pool, clerical section or print room.

This subject will be discussed further in the chapter on clerical work measurement.

6.4 Planning and cost controls

Many people, not associated with the planning of work, wonder how complex projects such as airliners, ships or intricate pieces of machinery are ever successfully built. However, there is no miracle about the completion of such feats. They result from the dovetailing of each of the individual tasks within the allotted time, using work measurement as the basis.

Elemental Breakdown. An element is defined (in British Standard 3138: 1969) as 'a distinct part of a specified job selected for convenience of observation, measurement and analysis'. Job breakdown is defined as 'a listing of the contents of a job by elements'. Elemental breakdown, then, is the division of a job into its constituent elements for the purpose of simplifying the task of observation, measurement, analysis and work planning. (Author's definition.)

In the manufacturing industries, the area of management dealing with the problems of planning may carry a title such as production planning and control. This is defined in the British Standard as 'procedures and means by which manufacturing programmes and plans are determined, information is issued for their execution and data is collected and recorded to control manufacture in accordance with the plans'.

However, before manufacturing programmes and plans can be determined, it is essential to carry out an elemental breakdown of the product through sub-divisions. Here is an example (in reverse order):

1. Testing the final product
2. Building of main assemblies into final product
3. Building of main assemblies from sub-assemblies

4. Building of main sub-assemblies
5. Building of sub-assemblies from (sub) sub-assemblies and constituent parts
6. Manufacture (and purchasing) of individual pieces, including decisions on:
   (i) made-in complete (from stock, standard materials)
   (ii) bought-out finished
   (iii) bought-out rough and manufactured in factory
   (iv) bought-out, part-finished and processed in factory

The position is hardly any different in an office situation and it may be just as complex a planning problem. For example, consider the nature of the paperwork systems controlling a joint project such as the Anglo-French Concorde. A similar procedure can be gone through for the production planning and control of paperwork as we have outlined above. In this case, of course, we are dealing with paperwork and paperwork systems.

Planners in administrative areas need to know the answers to such questions as:

1. The total standard time and the standard times for all processed work. For example, how long will it take to process (raise and mail off) 15 000 purchase orders?
2. How many people will be required, divided into sex, age groups and skills, to perform such work? For example, we may need to raise and mail off the 15 000 purchase orders each week.

Of course, planners will need to know much more than the answers to the above two questions, but these concern the time-content of work and are of direct concern to us here.

Time-basis of planning. If incentives are introduced in administrative areas, standard times can be used, based on anticipated (achievable) standard performance. Without any incentive element in this area, it is extremely unlikely that standard performance will be achieved, and the planner might have to fall back on the use of normal rating (75 on the British Standard 0/100 scale: see Figure 4.4 on page 51). The description of this rate is 'steady, deliberate, unhurried, under proper supervision: looks slow, but time not wasted when under observation'. It is clearly in a company's interests to aim to establish standard performance as the norm in their organization.

Once achievable time standards have been set, the information can be used by the planners for such immediate stages as:

1. Accurate time estimates for use in the construction of critical path networks (see Chapter 9). The object here is to take an accurate look at the overall planning of projects in order to meet required delivery dates.
2. Planning manpower requirements.
3. Planning space, machinery and equipment programmes.

4. Planning cost-control and budget programmes.

Labour control. Once a basis has been established for labour standards, it becomes a relatively straightforward matter to monitor performance. Some of the performance indices are listed here (based on British Standard 3138: 1969):

1. Operator performance: excluding any diverted time and waiting time, this index is obtained by calculating the following ratio:

$$\frac{\text{total standard times for all measured and estimated work}}{\text{time spent on measured and estimated work}} \times \frac{100}{1}$$

This may be considered as a true operator performance index

2. Departmental performance:

$$\frac{\text{total standard times for measured and estimated work}}{\text{time spent on measured and estimated work} + \text{any waiting time or diverted time for which the department is responsible}} \times \frac{100}{1}$$

3. Overall performance: this gives an indication of the net utilization of labour in producing the useful output:

$$\frac{\text{total productive standard times for measured and estimated work} + \text{productive uncontrolled work at assessed performance}}{\text{total attendance time} - \text{time spent on allocated work}} \times \frac{100}{1}$$

Uncontrolled work is defined as 'work for which no control standards have been determined' and allocated work is 'work for which control standards have been set by allocating a number of workers or working hours to support various levels of output. The work content of the work may not have been accurately determined.' Straightforward control documentation can be designed, based on these performance indices and these fall into groups, as follows:

1. Individual daily work (time) sheets, recording such information as job number, time taken, quantity, lost time, unmeasured and estimated times.
2. Sectional daily work sheets, grouping such information alongside work values in standard minutes: the responsibility for compiling and checking these is with the section leader.
3. Departmental daily work sheets: these are the responsibility of the departmental manager and all shortcomings should be explained or justified.

Management by exception. The control which can be exercised by standard costing operates on this principle. It consists of taking immediate action on reported exceptions to or variances from standard.

Applied work study principles—uses of work measurement

As there are many types of costs generated in a business, it becomes necessary to classify or separate costs into areas for control purposes. This follows the well-established and basic work study procedure of elemental breakdown.

Figure 6.2 shows a management by exception report on the work of a light-component assembly department in a factory employing one thousand people. The product had been fully work-measured and labour

Type	403 pump unit	Product assembly labour efficiency		
Department: Pump assembly		Week ending:		
Assembly section	Actual wages paid £	Budget wages £	Variance	Rectification work (included in column 2)
A	192	146	(46)	—
B	884	946	62	42
C	568	456	(112)	—
D	1011	1020	(10)	26
	£2688	£2576	£(112)	£68
Based on units passed to external (government) test			Total units: 4230	

Figure 6.2 Management by exception report

standards were well established on production lines staffed mostly by women. The figures shown in parentheses indicate adverse variances although on the actual documents these figures were printed in red ink, without the parentheses. The weekly report also gave the 'year to date' figures. Frequent reports of this type are a real help to management and in this case it is clearly their duty to investigate (and report on) the rectification work in sections B and D of the pump assembly department and investigate the adverse labour variances in sections A, C and D.

Cash emphasis. Supervisors meeting up with financial reporting systems for the first time may be surprised to find an emphasis on cash, rather than time. This is really the job of the accountant, to bring to everyone's notice the financial aspects of their individual contributions to the company effort, and their cash performance against previously agreed budgets and targets.

An interesting example of this emphasis is shown in Figure 6.3, which illustrates a simple control system for a small non-ferrous foundry in a light engineering company employing one thousand people. We see here the departmental operating statement for the foundry: a document such as this provides the framework for a useful control on the direct labour cost per pound of castings fettled (trimmed) and a close watch can be kept on such factors as waiting time. Supervisors will notice the almost exclusive use of cash figures where key information is recorded. Amongst the important information can be listed the all-important 'pence (of direct labour) per pound of metal' figure, direct workers' overtime hours (trends) and indirect workers' overtime hours (trends).

1. Labour cost incurred
   Direct labour
   Product A   Nil
   Product B   Nil
   Product C   £166.72

2. Fettled weight produced
   (light alloy) Metal 1 (weighting × 3) Nil
                  Metal 2   6945 lbs
                  Metal 3   Nil
                  Total equivalent weight = 6945 lbs

3. Direct labour cost per lb fettled
   (i) current week   2.4 pence per lb
   (ii) cumulative week 2.36 pence per lb

   Indirect labour

	Direct workers booking indirect	Indirect workers
A/c No. 100 Waiting time	Nil	Nil
104 Cleaning	£1.30	Nil
107 Training	Nil	Nil
108 Sundry indirect, day school, etc.	£0.34	£88.99
110 Overtime premium	£2.56	£6.96
	£4.20	£95.95

4. Personnel

	Direct labour	Indirect labour	Total labour force	Week plus or minus	Overtime hours Direct	Overtime hours Indirect
Male	9	5				
Female	3					
Total	12	5	17	+1	29	56

   Plus or minus +1
   Absent

Figure 6.3 Weekly departmental operating statement for • small, non-ferrous foundry

Labour variances. The two most important factors in most businesses, as far as labour is concerned, are the rate of pay of the workers and the efficiency with which the work is performed. As we have seen, standard costing discloses differences between expected and actual figures. Labour cost variances fall into the three categories of labour efficiency variance, labour rate variance and labour cost variance, all of which involve the use of standards.

Labour efficiency variance is expressed as

$$\left\{ \text{actual hours} - \text{standard hours for the actual output} \right\} \times \text{standard rate}$$

Applied work study principles—uses of work measurement 95

Labour rate variance is expressed as

(actual rate − standard rate) × actual number of hours

Labour cost variance is expressed as

(actual hours × actual rate) − (standards hours × standard rate)

Let us consider a labour variance example for a purchasing department. Clerical standard production data for raising a purchase order are as follows (standards per average order):

standard labour rate = 50 p/hour
standard hours = 1/6 hours per order raised (based on time study)
actual orders raised = 4000
actual labour rate = 56p/hour
actual hours worked = 600 (therefore less than required by standard which would be $\frac{4000}{6} = 666\frac{2}{3}$)

Using our formulae, we calculate in the following way:

1. Labour efficiency variance:

$$£\left(600 - \frac{4000}{6}\right) \times \frac{50}{100} = -£33\frac{1}{3} \text{ (favourable)}$$

2. Labour rate variance:

$$£(56-50)\frac{1}{100} \times 600 = +£36 \text{ (unfavourable)}$$

and answer 2 − answer 1 = £2⅔ (unfavourable)

3. Labour cost variance:

$$£\left\{600 \times \frac{56}{100}\right\} - £\left\{\frac{4000}{6} \times \frac{50}{100}\right\} = £336 - £\frac{2000}{6}$$
$$= +£2\frac{2}{3} \text{ (unfavourable)}$$

This agrees with the difference between the labour efficiency and rate variances above.

Material variances: A similar treatment can be given to the materials used, and material cost variances fall into three categories.

Material cost variance is expressed as

(actual quantity × actual price) − (standard quantity × standard price)

Material price variance is expressed as

(actual price − standard price) × actual quantity of material used

Material usage variance is expressed as

$$\left\{\begin{array}{l}\text{actual quantity} \\ \text{of material}\end{array} - \begin{array}{l}\text{standard quantity of material} \\ \text{for production achieved}\end{array}\right\} \times \text{standard price}$$

Making further use of our example of the purchasing department, we now have some additional information:

actual order (sets) used = 4100 (100 scrapped in typing)
standard cost of an order set = 5p
actual cost of an order set = 6p (due to poor buying or inefficiency in company's own printing department)

The calculations are as follows:

1. Material cost variance:

$$\frac{4100 \times 6}{100} - \frac{4000 \times 5}{100} = +£46 \text{ (unfavourable)}$$

2. Material price variance:

$$\frac{6-5}{100} \times 4100 = +£41 \text{ (unfavourable)}$$

3. Material usage variance:

$$(4100 - 4000) \times \frac{5}{100} = +£5 \text{ (unfavourable)}$$

The example quoted should serve to illustrate the general approach to cost control. Although labour costs will generally comprise the major part of total office costs, the costs of materials should not be ignored, since they can represent a considerable sum of money. O and M is certainly very interested in the reduction of material costs.

Examination questions

1. Why is it important to prepare a complete work specification? What items should be included?
   (City & Guilds *Work Study*, 1969)
2. State the advantages and disadvantages of financial incentives. Outline three different types of schemes, and describe in detail the operation of one of them.
   (IWSP *Incentives*, 1969)
3. Discuss the job of a line supervisor in a department with an incentive scheme based on measured work. Compare this situation with his job when operatives are paid time work rates.
   (IWSP *Incentives*, 1969)
4. When considering the introduction of a financial incentive scheme, what conditions would you prescribe to enable the best results to be achieved?
   (IWSP *Incentives*, 1968)

Applied work study principles—uses of work measurement

5. Explain what is meant by a measured daywork scheme. Under what conditions would you recommend the use of such a scheme?
    (IWSP *Incentives*, 1968)
6. In preparing a financial incentive scheme, what precautions should a work study officer recommend and take to avoid any increase in accidents?
    (City & Guilds *Work Study*, 1968)
7. Explain how the standard labour cost of a product or service is determined.
    (Part of IWSP Graduate Paper *Costing*, 1967)
8. Say to what extent a system of budgeting is necessary in the establishment of standard costs. Describe any similarities between standard costing and budgetary control.
    (IWSP Graduate *Costing*, 1967)
9. Discuss the use of work specifications in the development of operator training programmes.
    (IWSP *Industrial Relations*, 1973)
10. (i) What is a cost variance?
    (ii) A company manufactures one standard product. In a month in which the output was 1000, the actual costs were

direct materials used	£4500
direct wages paid	£6200
overheads incurred	£4200

    The standard cost is

direct materials	£5 per unit
direct wages	£6 per unit
overheads	£4 per unit

    Calculate the total cost variance.
    (iii) Give possible reasons for the direct material cost variance and the direct wages variance.
    (IWSP *Costing Aspects*, 1974)
11. (i) What is the purpose of determining cost variances?
    (ii) Describe the costing components used in the analysis of direct materials cost variance and also direct wages variance.
    (iii) Explain how unfavourable variances may arise
    (IWSP *Costing Aspects*, 1973)
12. Explain the role of costing, either by itself or in association with work study in the more efficient conduct of non-trading organizations.
    (IWSP *Costing Aspects*, 1973)
13. (i) What are the main purposes of a work specification when issuing a standard time?
    (ii) What information does a work specification usually include?
    (IWSP *Work Measurement—Technical and Clerical*, 1974)

14. Explain the meaning and purpose of the following:
    (i) direct wages variance
    (ii) direct wages rate variance
    (iii) direct labour efficiency variance
    (IWSP *Costing Aspects*, 1972)
15. Explain the nature of standard costs and how they may be related to budgets.
    (Institution of Works Managers, college paper)
16. What are the relevant advantages and disadvantages of payment by day rates and piece rates?
    (Institution of Works Managers, college paper)
17. (i) What is a multi-factor scheme?
    (ii) Give an example of a situation in which this method of payment would be appropriate.
    (City & Guilds *Work Study*, 1974)
18. Give the reasons why management may seek a change from using individual incentive schemes.
    (City & Guilds *Work Study*, 1974)
19. What are the essential differences between a measured day-work scheme and a graded performance scheme? What do you consider to be the main advantages and disadvantages of each type of scheme?
    (City & Guilds *Work Study*, 1973)

7
Applied work study principles—method study charting

Before discussing method study charting, it will be useful to repeat our definition of method study: 'The systematic recording and critical examination of the factors and resources involved in existing and proposed ways of doing work, as a means of developing and applying easier and more effective methods and reducing costs'.

In the eight-stage work study procedure discussed in Chapter 4, we saw that Stage 2 was the Record stage, which led on to the Examine and Develop stages. One of the most useful techniques for recording activities is the method study chart. It has the following clear advantages:
1. It is a visible, graphical form of explanation. People generally appreciate pictures more readily than figures.
2. Present and proposed methods of doing the same job can be very clearly presented side by side.
3. This presentation stimulates both the recorder and the other people involved to fill in missing pieces of information.

7.1 Process-sequence charts

As we are almost inevitably involved in a work process, whether it be on the shop floor or in the office, the method study process chart is a very useful type of recording technique. Some definitions from British Standard BS 3138: 1969 will be useful here. Process charts themselves are defined as 'charts in which a sequence of events is portrayed diagrammatically by means of a set of process chart symbols to help a person to visualize a process as a means of examining and improving it'. Readers should particularly note that the process chart has the same basic purpose as method study itself, to develop more effective methods (improvements) and reduce costs.

Outline process chart. This is 'a process chart giving an overall picture by recording in sequence only the operations and inspections'. Part of such a

① Open envelopes (extract invoices)

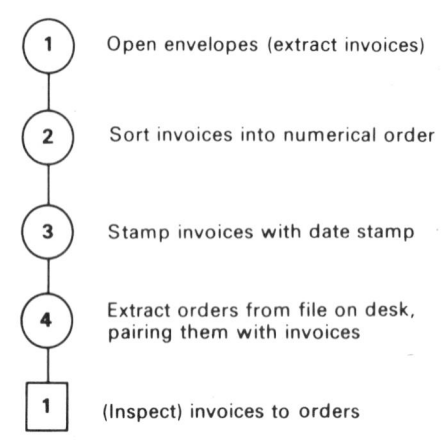

② Sort invoices into numerical order

③ Stamp invoices with date stamp

④ Extract orders from file on desk, pairing them with invoices

□ 1 (Inspect) invoices to orders

Figure 7.1 Part of an outline process chart for a clerical procedure

process chart for a clerical procedure is illustrated in Figure 7.1. We are introducing two symbols at this stage:

INSPECTION □ Indicates an inspection for quality and/or a check quantity.

OPERATION ○ Indicates the main steps in a process, method or procedure. Usually the part, material or product concerned is modified or changed during the operation.

We should note that the numbering of each type of symbol follows on in sequence and is individual to each type of symbol.

Flow process chart. This is defined as 'a process chart setting out the sequence of the flow of a product or a procedure by recording all events under review using the appropriate process chart symbols'. There are three types of flow process chart:

1. Man type—'a flow process chart which records what the worker does'.
2. Material type—'a flow process chart which records what happens to material'.
3. Equipment type—'a flow process chart which records how the equipment is used'.

Part of such a process chart for a clerical procedure is illustrated in Figure 7.2. Four new symbols have been introduced, and are defined as follows:

TRANSPORT: ⇦ Indicates the movement of workers, materials or equipment from place to place.

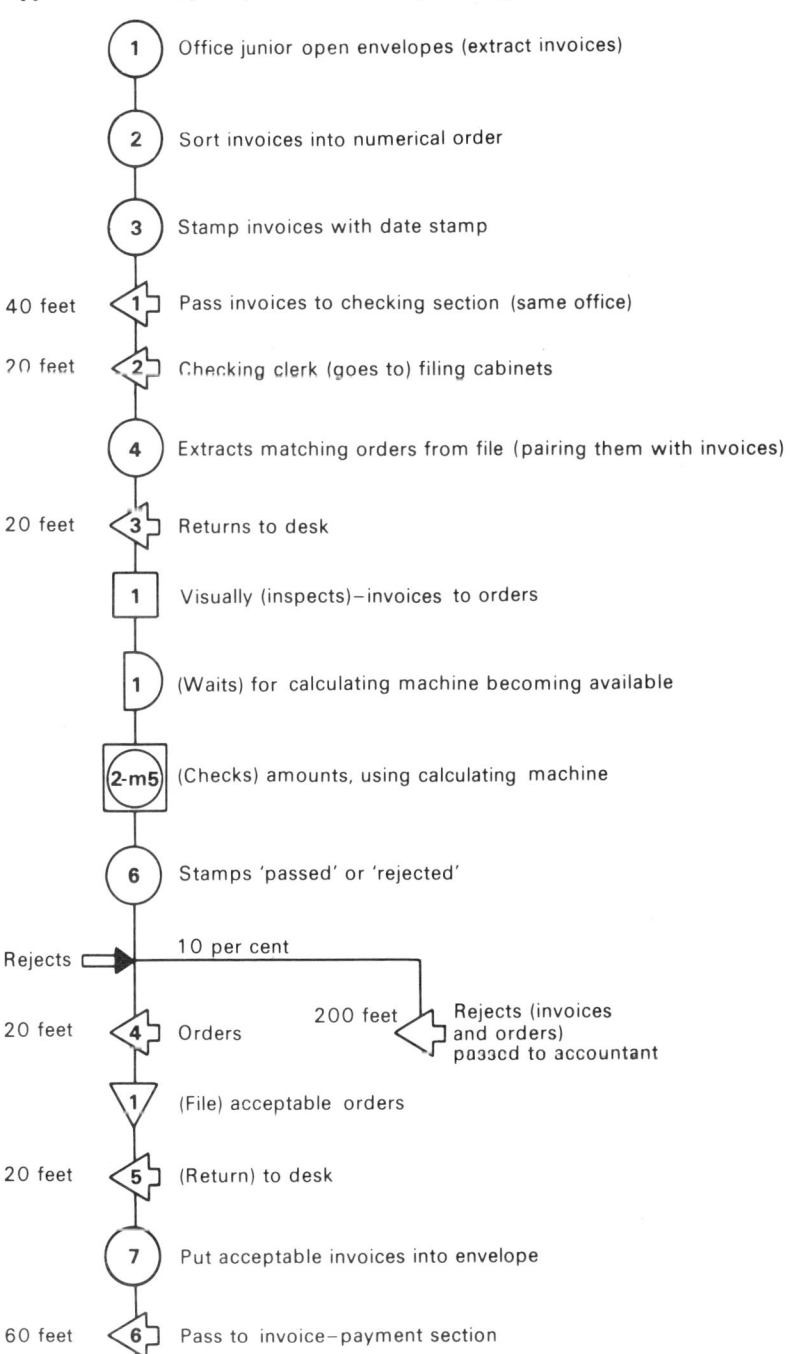

Applied work study principles—method study charting 101

	① Office junior open envelopes (extract invoices)
	② Sort invoices into numerical order
	③ Stamp invoices with date stamp
40 feet	▷1 Pass invoices to checking section (same office)
20 feet	▷2 Checking clerk (goes to) filing cabinets
	④ Extracts matching orders from file (pairing them with invoices)
20 feet	▷3 Returns to desk
	□1 Visually (inspects)–invoices to orders
	①(Waits) for calculating machine becoming available
	▣2-m5 (Checks) amounts, using calculating machine
	⑥ Stamps 'passed' or 'rejected'
Rejects ⇨	10 per cent
	200 feet ▷ Rejects (invoices and orders) passed to accountant
20 feet	▷4 Orders
	▽1 (File) acceptable orders
20 feet	▷5 (Return) to desk
	⑦ Put acceptable invoices into envelope
60 feet	▷6 Pass to invoice–payment section

Figure 7.2 Flow process chart for a clerical procedure

TEMPORARY STORAGE OR DELAY: ▽(D-shape)

Indicates a delay in the sequence of events; for example, work or worker waiting between consecutive operations or any object laid aside temporarily without record until required.

PERMANENT STORAGE ▽

Indicates a controlled storage in which material is received into or issued from a store under some form of authorization or an item is retained for reference purposes.

REJECTS

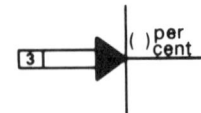

Indicates a point in a process where a rejection takes place (for example, broken crockery in a pottery factory). The reject number is shown and also the percentage rejected. (This is *not* from BS 3138.)

In addition, a combined symbol has been used:

COMBINED SYMBOL

The main activity is indicated by the outside symbol, that is Inspection. At the same time, an operation is carried out (such as stamping with a number), in this case a machine operation (machine indicated by M). The numbering system follows the rule that the first number relates to the major activity. Thus, Inspection No. 2 and (machine) operation No. 5. (This is *not* from BS 3138.)

In the above example, if there are a number of machine operations, the observer may wish to number these separately, as distinct from manual operations. In any case, a key should always be supplied with a process chart.

Note: a clerical operation *could* be indicated by:

Two-handed process chart. The definition reads 'a process chart in which the activities of a worker's hands (or limbs) are recorded in relationship to one another'. As an example, we might consider an office order-typist sitting at desk, hands on desk, directly in front: the chart is given in Figure 7.3.

This type of process chart is usually reserved for the study of highly repetitive work, where small reductions in the cycle time are worthwhile due to the large number of cycles performed. There are many such operations in offices.

Other symbols. If the product *changes its state*, for example, liquid soap is solidified into a bar, it may be shown as in Figure 7.4.

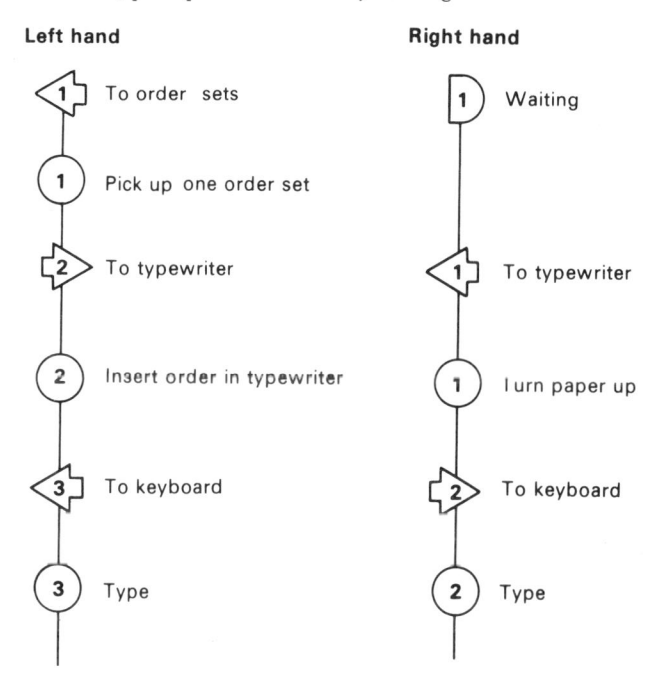

Applied work study principles—method study charting 103

Left hand   **Right hand**

Left hand	Right hand
⇨1 To order sets	1 Waiting
1 Pick up one order set	
⇨2 To typewriter	⇨1 To typewriter
2 Insert order in typewriter	1 Turn paper up
⇨3 To keyboard	⇨2 To keyboard
3 Type	2 Type

Figure 7.3 Two-handed process chart for typing operation

There is also a symbol for *alternative processes*. If a product can travel through different process lines, depending upon its individual circumstances, it can be recorded as in Figure 7.5. For example, shirts could pass along a production line until a certain stage in making up and then separate into lines for sub-standard and special (with fancy additions).

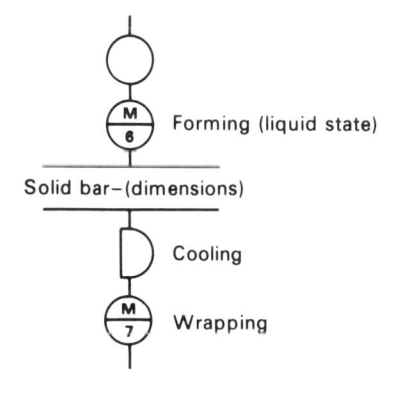

○
Ⓜ6 Forming (liquid state)
———————————
Solid bar—(dimensions)
———————————
▽ Cooling
Ⓜ7 Wrapping

Figure 7.4 Method of showing a change of state

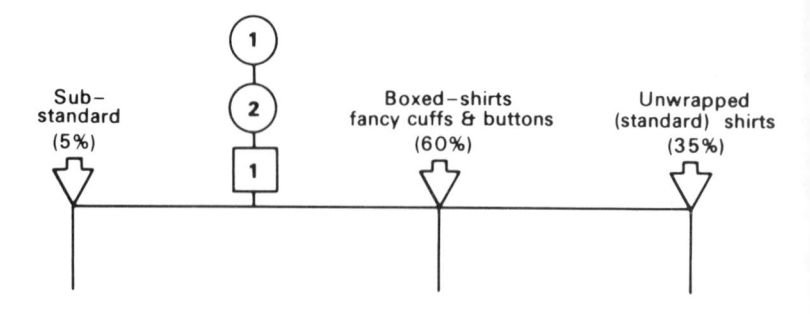

Figure 7.5 Method of showing alternative processes

Figure 7.6 illustrates the use of *alternative routes* symbolization to describe the production of tablets. Notice that (machine) operations 3 and 4 are given separate numbers because they are quite different

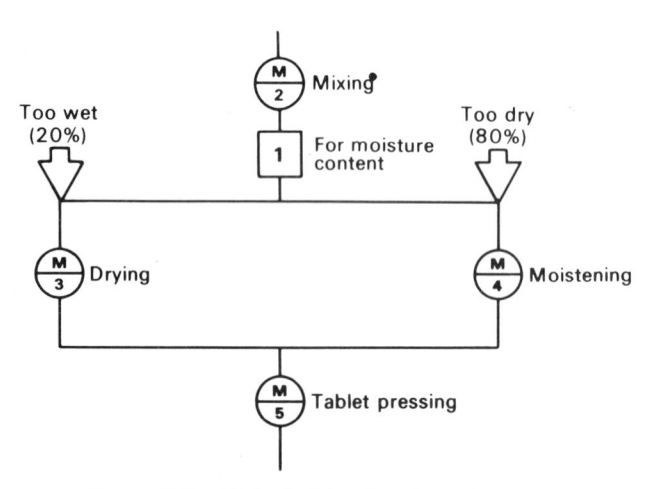

Figure 7.6 Method of showing alternative routes

operations, having different work contents. In the case shown in Figure 7.7 (illustrating *multi-manning*) a product is machine-produced at M-2 and the work content of the next stage is such that two (identical) machines are required to keep up with its output. Therefore the two operations at this stage must carry the same number (M3). A group of girls then hand-pack the product at operation 8. It is permissible to use the symbols M3(a) and M3(b).

From the symbols shown in Figure 7.8, we see that the machine operation M-6 spoils some parts, but a percentage of them are *rectified* on a hand line, so that they may be passed to the next machine operation (M-7).

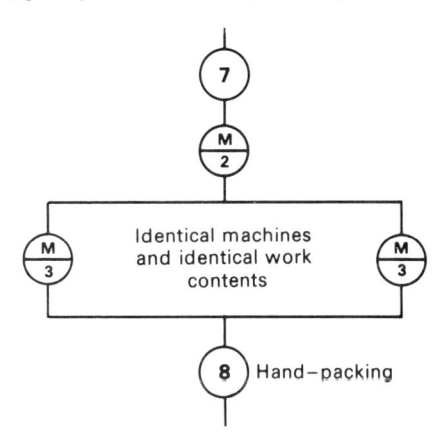

Applied work study principles—method study charting

Figure 7.7 Method of showing multi-manning

However, if the same percentage has passed through the M 6 stage but the machine has not performed its function at all, then the line from the reject point could pass back and enter the production line on the chart at a point between operation 8 and M-6 (*re-cycling*). In practice, it may not be convenient to break into a machine feed and re-cycling may not be the best answer.

Figure 7.9 illustrates the symbols used to indicate *entry of parts or materials*.

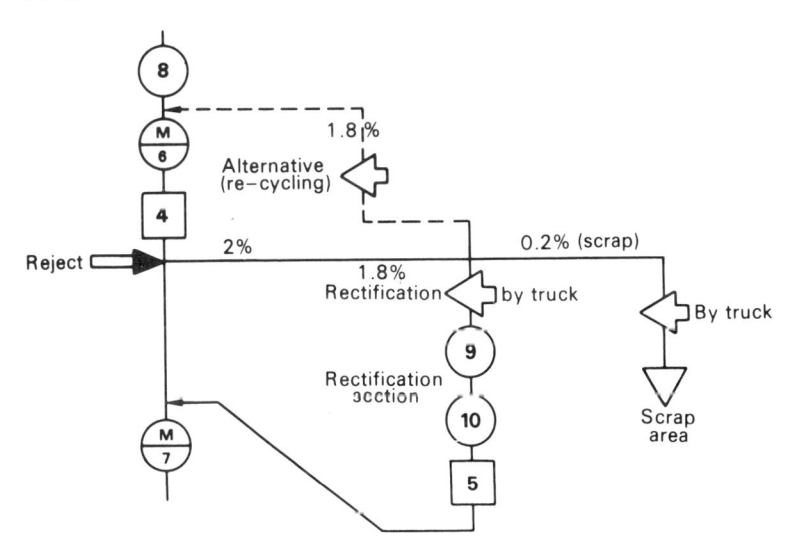

Figure 7.8 Method of showing rectification and re-cycling

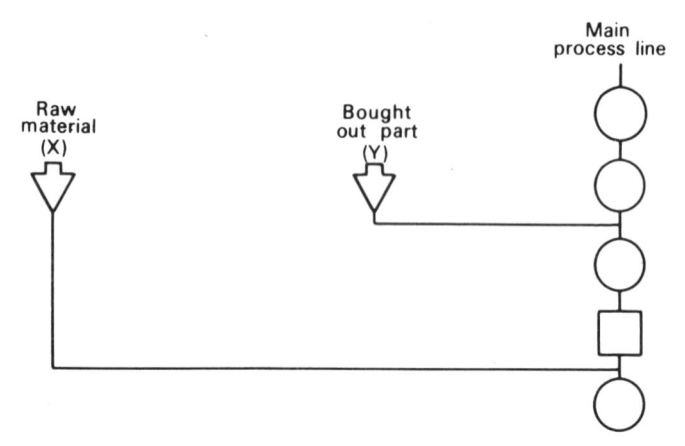

Figure 7.9 Method of showing entry of parts or materials

Summary table and key. A summary table should be included at the foot of every process chart. Since the fundamental idea of method study is to discover a better, more economical way of doing a job, the process chart for the better method should be presented alongside a process chart showing the current method. The summary table should then take the form shown in Figure 7.10. Every process chart should also have a key to the symbolization used: it is not good enough to assume that others will automatically understand what is meant.

Exercise in Process Charting. Readers will benefit from drawing a process chart to describe the following manufacturing process. A large piece of plain paper is suggested (A3 or A2 size). Figure 7.11 shows a reproduction of a template that can be useful when drawing process charts.

A firm manufactures a brand of boiled sweets to a standard pattern up to a point in production irrespective of the customer presentation required. The last three operations, before selective preparation, are
1. Form sweets (machine).
2. Wrap (machine).
3. Inspect (on conveyor) for faulty sweets or wrappings; reject (2 per cent) from line but bag these in plastic bags for cheap sale; send to dispatch bay by truck.

Remaining procedure is as follows:
4. 20 per cent of sweets are packed into christmas boxes for storage (machine), then wrapped, inspected and sent to special store by truck.
5. 30 per cent of sweets are packed in 4-ounce plastic bags (machine) and then packed in cardboard boxes. They are subsequently labelled according to destination:

Applied work study principles—method study charting   107

		Present method		Proposed method
◯		26		12
▢		10		10
▽		12		8
◁	24	Total distance 4200 feet	14	Total distance 1600 feet
D		10		6
TOTALS		82		50

Figure 7.10   Process chart summary table

  50 per cent (of 30 per cent) red label
  30 per cent blue label
  20 per cent green label
  Green-label boxes are specially weatherproofed after labelling. Inspection then takes place (labels and box-security). Then boxes go via conveyor to dispatch, to temporary pallet storage.
6. 40 per cent of sweets are packed in christmas stockings (machine), inspected and then sent by truck to the special store.
7. 10 per cent are packed in bottles (machine) and then capped on a separate machine; 0.05 per cent of bottles are broken at packing stage and 0.1 per cent suffer broken plastic bottle caps. The latter bottles are passed to a top-refitting station. Bottles pass to a labelling machine. 0.04 per cent are broken at this stage. Inspection takes place for label position and security of top, but 0.1 per cent

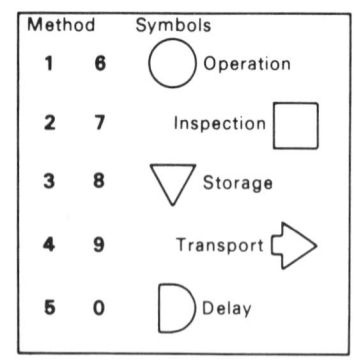

Method		Symbols
1	6	◯ Operation
2	7	Inspection ▢
3	8	▽ Storage
4	9	Transport ⇨
5	0	⟂ Delay

SOURCE: Quickdraw, London W3.

Figure 7.11 Method study symbol template

require correction before passing to conveyor (60 per cent require new label fitting and 40 per cent require top tightening). Then via conveyor to dispatch and temporary pallet storage.

Note: all scrap is taken by truck to temporary storage in a scrap area.

Draw a flow process chart, describing in detail the activities given and number the symbols used. Draw up a summary table of the symbols used.

7.2 Movement charts

String Diagram. This is 'a scale plan or model on which a thread is used to trace and measure the path of workers, materials or equipment during a specified sequence of events'. The following equipment is required to make such a useful chart: a flat board or open-sided model with removable floors (in the case of a multi-storey building); spherical-headed pins, preferably coloured; coloured thread (different colours); large sheets of white paper on which to draw a plan of the area being studied.

The outstanding advantage of this type of chart is that a complex present method is strikingly presented and a much-simplified proposed method is shown to the very best advantage in comparison. The string diagram is a very useful technique to use in the planning of new facilities and should produce sound materials handling.

Travel Chart. This is defined as 'a tabular record for presenting quantitative data about the movements of workers, materials or equipment between any number of places over any given period of time'. The example shown in Figure 7.12 is a travel chart recording the number of callers from one department to another (taking mail and general information). For example, five calls are made by sales department personnel to the production department and only two calls are made by production department personnel to the sales department.

Applied work study principles—method study charting 109

There are other types of travel charts, to suit various needs: we will look briefly at four of them.

1. The distance-type travel chart is the same as the travel chart shown except that, instead of recording frequencies in the spaces provided, the distances between respective departments are recorded.
2. The weighted-factor travel chart is the same as the previous chart except that, instead of a straight footage being recorded, factors of

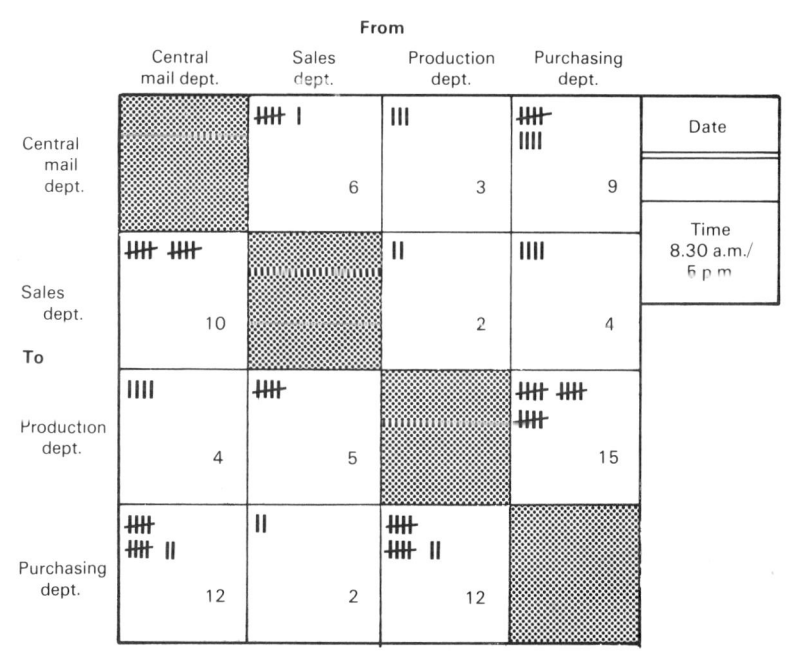

Figure 7.12 Travel chart: callers from department to department

some kind are calculated and inserted in the appropriate spaces. Features taken into consideration during an office-study could include the distance between departments, the volume of paperwork and the importance of the traffic. It is appreciated that some of this is subjective: for instance, how is importance measured? In practice, managers should be challenged to make the mental effort to agree on a scale. It can be done.

3. The proximity chart is similar to the distance-type of travel chart, but instead of recording distances between departments, a proximity-code is inserted in each of the boxes. This could be based on the priority for proximity and the reasons for such priorities. For example, let us suppose that we have a numerical code for proximity

and that 1 indicates that two departments should be adjacent, such as the materials control department and the purchasing department. Let us also suppose that the reason for desiring proximity in this case, is that there is a heavy flow of paperwork between these departments, indicated by B on a lettered scale for reasons. The entry would then read

	materials control department
purchasing department	1B

This type of chart is of great importance when planning a new factory, for example.

4. Finally, we have the topographical movement chart. The particularly useful feature of this type of chart is that distances between points of interest are recorded to scale on a piece of paper. Superimposed on to the lines drawn between departments having inter-related work are figures recording levels of activity. For example, the chart in Figure 7.13 shows a central department (A) and three other departments, with walking distances between them drawn to scale. The figures

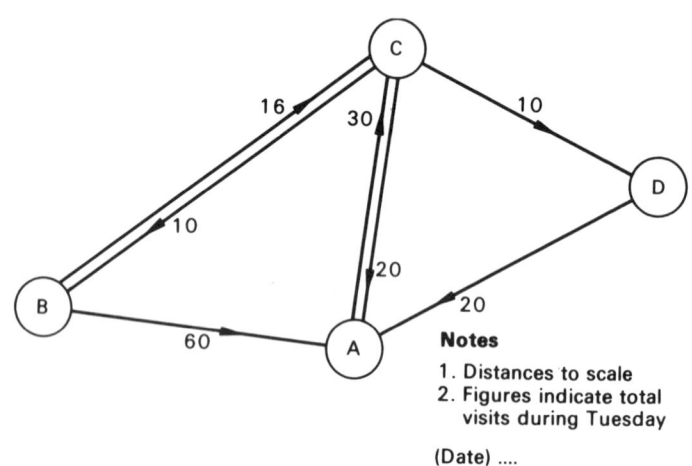

Figure 7.13 Topographical movement chart

represent the number of visits made by the personnel of the respective departments to other departments. Personnel from department A made thirty visits to department C on the day in question and personnel from department C made twenty visits to department A. None of department A's personnel visited departments B and D. Again, this is a useful technique when planning new facilities.

Applied work study principles—method study charting 111

Flow diagram. This is defined as 'a diagram or model, substantially to scale, which shows the location of specific activities carried out and the routes followed by workers, materials or equipment. Process chart symbols may be embodied in the diagram.' This chart is similar to the string diagram but the addition of process chart symbols is particularly helpful on occasions. The example shown in Figure 7.14 records the

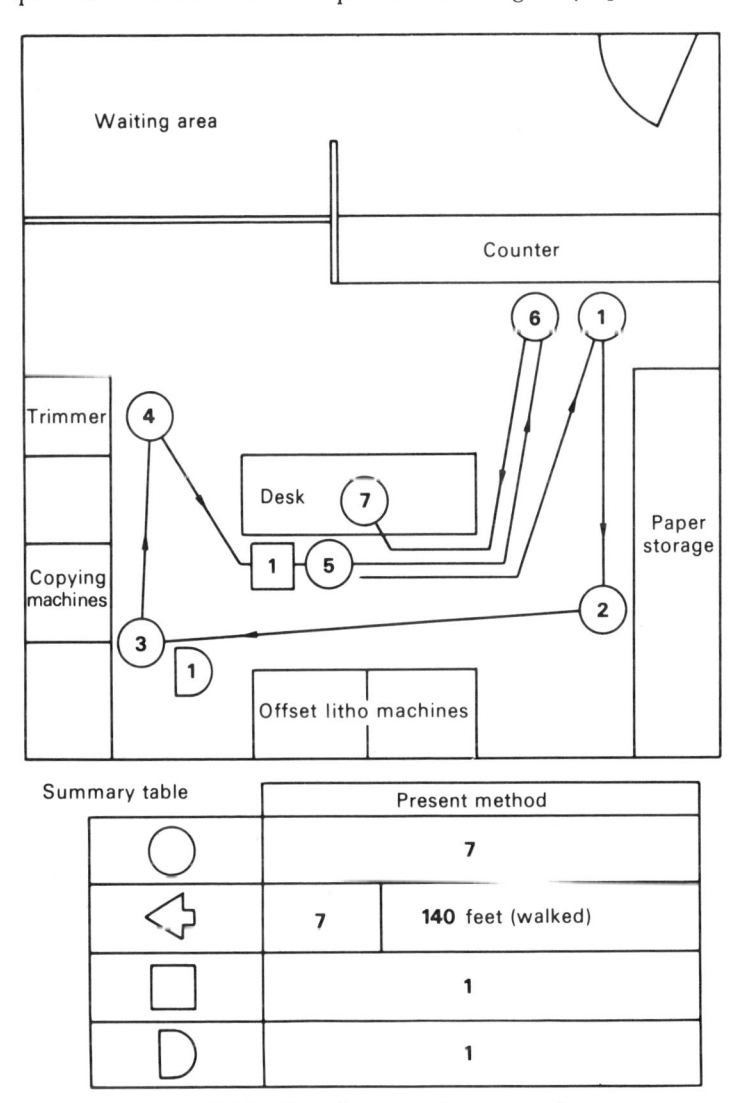

Summary table		Present method
○		7
⇦	7	140 feet (walked)
□		1
D		1

Figure 7.14 Flow diagram: a photocopying bureau

activities and movements of an assistant in a bureau supplying a photocopying service. The assistant moves from her desk to the counter, takes and writes the order, makes the photocopies, checks the prices at her desk, writes the prices on an invoice and calculates the total price, returns to the counter, receives payment and finally sits at the desk and files the copy order.

7.3 Time-scale charts

One of the best-known and widely-used charts, using a time scale, is illustrated in Figure 7.15. It is the *multiple activity chart*, 'a chart on which the activities of more than one subject (worker, equipment or material) are each recorded on a common time scale to show their inter-relationship'.

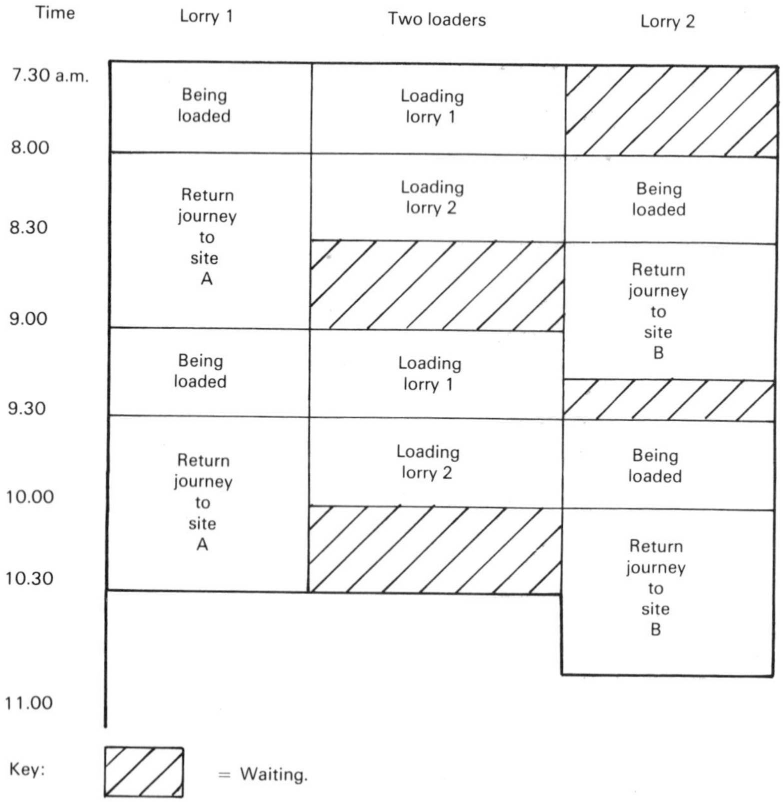

Time	Lorry 1	Two loaders	Lorry 2
7.30 a.m. – 8.00	Being loaded	Loading lorry 1	Waiting
8.00 – 8.30	Return journey to site A	Loading lorry 2	Being loaded
8.30 – 9.00	Return journey to site A	Waiting	Return journey to site B
9.00 – 9.30	Being loaded	Loading lorry 1	Waiting
9.30 – 10.00	Return journey to site A	Loading lorry 2	Being loaded
10.00 – 10.30	Return journey to site A	Waiting	Return journey to site B

Key: ▨ = Waiting.

Figure 7.15 Multiple activity chart: lorry loading

Applied work study principles—method study charting 113

The example shown here deals with a team of two men loading sand into two lorries at a quarry. Lorry 1 delivers to a site (A) which is a one-hour return journey and lorry 2 delivers to site (B) which is a forty-five minute return journey. The men take thirty minutes to load one lorry. It can be seen from examination of the chart that the two men are idle for a total of one hour between the hours of 7.30 and 10.30 a.m., which constitutes an actual idle time of two man-hours. Lorry 2 is also waiting (together with its driver) for forty-five minutes. The purpose of the multiple activity chart is to discover such time wastage and to design better schedules.

7.4 Miscellaneous charts

It now remains to describe three charts which are very useful in O and M work.

Paperwork procedure narrative. This is a written account of the consecutive steps in a procedure, relating to the person, activity and detail. Figure 7.16 is an example, showing the commencement of a paperwork procedure narrative for the receipt and payment of invoices.

Receipt and payment of invoices (Invoice-payment section)					
Method:	Present	Date:		Observer:	
Person	Activity		Details		
Office junior	Opens		envelopes	
	Extracts		invoices	
	Sorts		invoices into numerical order	
	Stamps		invoices using date stamp	
	Takes		invoices to checking section	
Check clerk	Takes		invoice stack to filing cabinets	

Figure 7.16 Paperwork procedure narrative

Paperwork procedure chart. This is a method of visually recording the path taken by the various documents in a procedure. It could be described as a paperwork-procedure route map. Two characteristics of this type of chart should be noted:

1. There is no record of the work carried out at any stage in the procedure.
2. There is no effort to record the documents receiving immediate attention and the documents receiving little attention (or, in fact, merely filed).

In Figure 7.17 we have an extract from a paperwork procedure chart for a works order/acknowledgement of order in an engineering company: this type of chart is sometimes known as a forms flow chart or a paperwork flow chart.

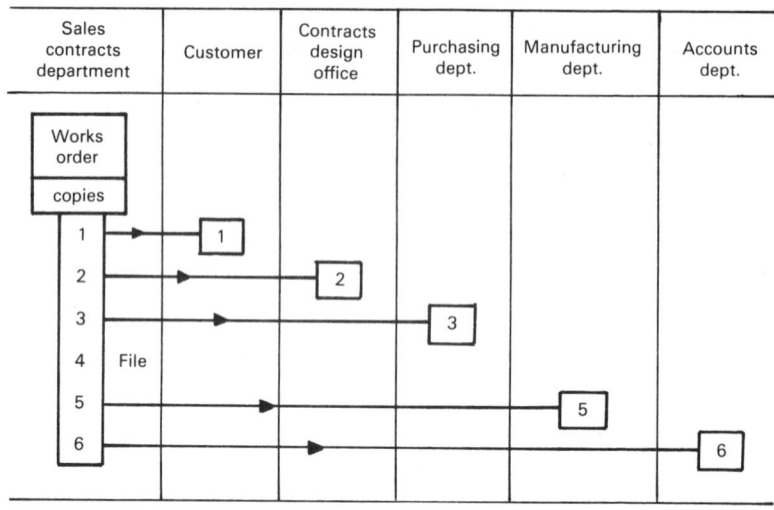

Sales contracts department	Customer	Contracts design office	Purchasing dept.	Manufacturing dept.	Accounts dept.
Works order copies 1 2 3 4 File 5 6		1 2	3	5	6

Figure 7.17 Paperwork procedure chart

Paperwork specimen chart. This is a collection of the various forms used in a procedure, mounted (in order of appearance) on a backing sheet. It is convenient for a number of reasons:

1. A total procedure can be seen at a glance, from the point of view of the actual forms.
2. A vivid impression can be gained of the complexity of paperwork systems, as a spur to simplifying them.
3. The backing sheet can be hung on a wall for group-discussion purposes.
4. It can be carried to meetings.
5. It can be photographed and prints circulated.

Figure 7.18 is an example of such a chart, using the works order discussed in the previous paragraph.

Readers should never forget the purpose of a chart. It should explain clearly what is happening or what should happen, the symbolism should be simple and a key should be provided. A sound charting procedure should encourage others to contribute information to the chart. It is a fact that many management personnel have lost touch with the detailed procedures in their own departments, due to pressure of work, enforced absence and the speed of change. The well-constructed chart can therefore be a welcome refresher.

Examination questions

1. Suppose you have been given the job of surveying the paperwork systems in use in an organization with a view to their improvement.

Applied work study principles—method study charting

    (i) Describe how you would set about the task.
    (ii) Outline the provisions you would suggest for the maintenance of the improvements you recommend.
                                                  (NEBSS Certificate, 1968)

2. Describe the principal ways used to record the facts during a method study assignment. Give an example of the use of one of them.
                                                  (City & Guilds *Work Study*, 1968)

3. Give an assumed example of an outline process chart involving an assembly job where two component parts join the principal unit at different stages in the sequence of operations. State for what purpose such a chart would be used.
                                                  (IWSP Graduate *Method Study*, 1967)

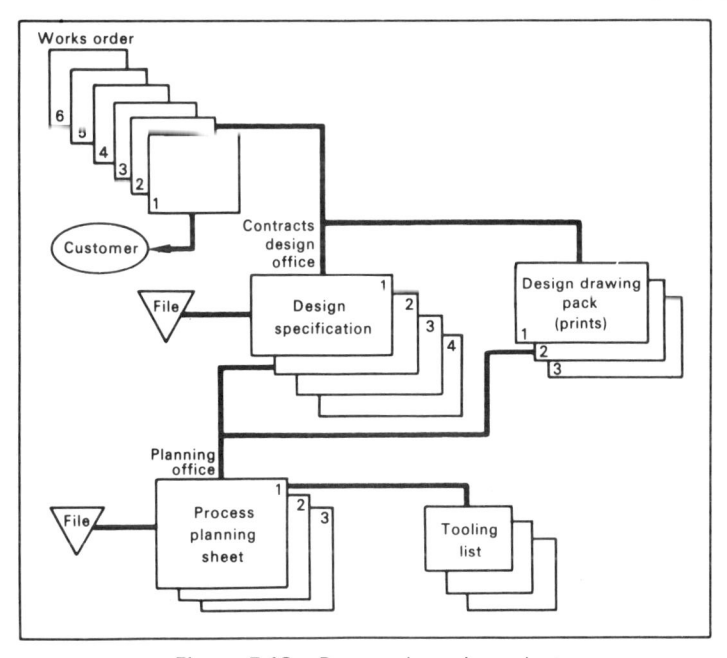

Figure 7.18   Paperwork specimen chart

4. In what way does an O and M paperwork flow chart differ from a flow process chart—material type? Illustrate the answer by drawing a paperwork flow chart for a simple office procedure involving at least three departments.
                                   (IWSP Graduate *Associated Techniques (A)*, 1969)

5. In what circumstances would you make use of a multiple activity chart and what would you expect to gain from its use? Give an example.
                                                  (IWSP Graduate *Method Study*, 1968)

6. Discuss the step 'record' in the basic procedure of method study, giving reasons for recording all the facts. Describe, briefly, three types of process charts, indicating clearly the application in each case.
(IWSP Graduate *Method Study*, 1969)
7. Construct a multiple activity chart showing the activities of one man controlling two machines. Complete the calculations to show the percentage utilization of man and machines.
(IWSP Graduate *Work Measurement*, 1969)
8. Outline the uses of each of the following when applied to the study of clerical activities:
   (i) flow diagram
   (ii) procedure map
   (iii) string diagram
   (iv) two-handed process chart
(IWSP *Method Study—Technical and Clerical*, 1974)
9. Describe two of the following recording methods:
   (i) procedure narrative
   (ii) procedure map
   (iii) flow diagram
   Of those methods selected, state fully their purpose and give simple examples of their use.
(IWSP *Method Study—Technical and Clerical*, 1972)
10. Under what circumstances and for what reasons would each of the following be used in an office situation:
    (i) activity sampling
    (ii) outline process chart
    (iii) multiple activity chart
    (iv) two-handed process chart
(IWSP *Method Study—Technical and Clerical*, 1973)

8
Clerical work measurement

8.1 Definitions

Clerical work measurement must be defined within the context of O and M and it should first be remembered that work measurement really divides into two areas of techniques. Firstly, there is time study, characterized by an observer using a time recording device such as a stop-watch and some subjective concept of performance rating, leading to data analysis and the setting of standards. Secondly, there are other techniques, such as activity sampling, predetermined motion time system (PMTS), synthesis and estimating.

Filming techniques, such as micromotion and memotion photography, and simultaneous motion cycle charts (Simo charts) are normally regarded as method study techniques. Indeed they are, more often than not, associated with the search for methods improvement. However, mention is made of them here because they permanently record activities on an absolutely accurate time scale: in fact, they often do so with greater accuracy than could an observer using a stop-watch. They can, of course, be quite expensive techniques to use.

It is probably true to say that, when O and M was first defined, the application of conventional time study to office procedures was not envisaged, at least not in the sense that time study was envisaged for shop floor applications.

Time study This is defined in British Standard (3138:1969) as 'a work measurement technique for recording the times and rates of working for the elements of a specified job carried out under specified conditions, and for analyzing the data so as to determine the time necessary for carrying out the job at a determined level of performance'.

Activity sampling. We have already defined this in an earlier chapter, but repetition here will avoid the need for turning back the pages: 'a technique in which a large number of observations are made over a period of time of one or a group of machines, processes or workers. Each observation records what is happening at that instant and the percentage of observations recorded for a particular activity or delay is a measure of the percentage of time during which that activity or delay occurs.' *Rated activity sampling* is a subdivision and is defined as 'an extension of activity sampling in which rating is applied so that where the frequency is known, work content may be established in addition to the proportion of time occupied by other activities or delays'.

PMTS. The definition reads: 'a work measurement technique whereby times established for basic human motions (classified according to the nature of the motion and the conditions under which it is made) are used to build up the time for a job at a defined level of performance'.

Synthesis. This is defined as 'a work measurement technique for building up the time for a job or parts of a job at a defined level of performance by totalling element times obtained previously from time studies on other jobs containing the elements concerned, or from synthetic data'.

Estimating. This is defined as 'a means for assessing the time required to carry out work, based on knowledge and experience of similar types of work, without a detailed breakdown of the work into elements and their corresponding times at a defined level of performance'. It is convenient to subdivide this further into *analytical estimating*: 'a work measurement technique, being a development of estimating, whereby the time required to carry out elements of a job at a defined level of performance is estimated partly from knowledge and practical experience of the elements concerned and partly from synthetic data' and *comparative estimating*: 'a work measurement technique, in which the time for a job is evaluated by comparing the work in it with the work in a series of similar jobs (benchmarks), the work content of which has been measured. The arranging of jobs into broad bands of time is referred to as slotting.'

Clerical work measurement can now be simply defined as follows: 'the application of work measurement techniques, including time study, to administrative areas of an organization in order to establish the time for a qualified worker to complete a specified job at a defined level of performance.' (Author's definition, with acknowledgements to British Standard 3138)

8.2 The need

It is now commonly held that there is an increased need for greater productivity and reduced costs in administrative areas. There has undoubtedly been a need for work measurement in the 'office' since offices existed, but emphasis was restricted to shop floor (predominantly manual) work, for a number of reasons:

1. The manpower emphasis, in the early days of industry, was on the manual (shop floor) side.
2. Before the effects of mechanization and automation were felt, large

Clerical work measurement

areas of manual work were not machine-assisted, necessitating the employment of many manual workers. This is seen, for example, in the work of F. W. Taylor (1856–1915) during his famous studies at the Bethlehem Steel Works, where he studied six hundred men shovelling raw materials.

3. The greater variability of office work and its 'thinking content' influenced many people in management to believe that this type of work could not be effectively measured.
4. Inevitably, there would be some senior management personnel who would feel that management techniques scrutiny was coming rather close to home if they encouraged the infiltration of work measurement into the administrative area.
5. There is a shortage of practitioners of the correct calibre, training and experience to make clerical work measurement really succeed, coupled with the wholehearted support of their senior managements.

The increased need for clerical work measurement, as defined, can again be ascribed to a number of reasons:

1. Increased automation in manufacturing areas tends to reduce the numbers of direct (manual) workers and to increase the number of indirect workers.
2. The increased complexity of administrative work threatens to weaken control because of the lack of accurate standards.
3. The increased emphasis on overhead costs in those companies carrying considerable research and development (and other) overhead costs and having dangerously high break-even percentages, in a general inflationary background.

8.3 Special problems

Paperwork problems. Office work is mainly concerned with the handling, processing, filing and transmission of documents. This is in direct contrast to a shop floor manufacturing area, where a visible, functional product is developing through the various stages of a production process. An error at a production stage may be quickly detected and easily measured. For example, a piece will not subsequently fit together with a mating part or a holding-fixture for the next operation. An error in paperwork may easily pass detection and the implications may be very serious indeed, especially when the paperwork is part of the input to a computer. An example of this occurs in the goods inward area, where a materials control computer is dependent upon accurate feedback paperwork, without being able to check the accuracy of the quantities recorded as received.

Paperwork problems are involved with the sheer quantity of matter circulating in an organization and the multiplicity of copies spun off from originating documents. Inevitably, such large quantities create filing and storage problems, not to mention the labour required to handle them.

Information flow. Paperwork can best be regarded as an information flow system and one cannot see information in the same sense as a product can be seen. Information contained in paperwork only springs to life when that information is acted upon. It gives authority to proceed and authority to commit company resources.

The organizational structure of a company is really a complex communications network and the office supervisor is often at one of the centres of such a network. The efficiency of an organization is a direct reflection of the response-sensitivity of the communications system. Information must flow accurately and swiftly, if management decisions are to be effectively implemented and time is of the essence. As an example, we might consider a standard costing reporting system. Variances from materials and labour standards must be reported to manufacturing management as rapidly as possible: it is vital that this information is accurate. Again, stock figures must be reported accurately and rapidly to the purchasing department if orders for replenishments are to be placed in good time.

Communications systems. The flow of information through an organization is inevitably linked with sophisticated communications equipment, such as:

telephone systems
teleprinter
telex
telegrams
dictating and transcription machines (for typed work)
intercom systems
closed circuit television
video-tape
telephone answering machines
document copying machines
radio-telephones
facsimile-telegraphy
document conveyors
gravity chutes
staff location systems
pneumatic tubes for document transmission

It follows that any project work undertaken in an office area should take special note of communications aspects. A proposed new system must fit in with existing systems and must also justify its cost.

Thinking time. In shop floor areas it is often easy for a work study observer to distinguish between 'working' and 'not working' classifications. This is not so in office areas.

It is important to decide what constitutes 'not working' for an office

Clerical work measurement

worker. If we consider a ledger clerk, for example, it would be an unwise decision to regard any of his time at the desk when he was not actually putting pen to paper as idle time. The observer must ascertain how much thinking and calculating time is involved before making an entry in the ledger: he may even need to make specimen calculations himself. Experienced observers in office areas will look principally for new methods of work. Activity sampling is a powerful tool in experienced hands and the most useful application will be to list all the duties carried out in the office area in question and to give a fair idea of the amount of time spent on each duty. However, once the main labour-consuming tasks in an office have been identified through activity sampling, certain of them may lend themselves to time study and possibly an incentive scheme.

Spread of activities. It is extremely important, in office studies, for consideration to be given to the spread of departmental duties over the calendar year. Wherever possible, studies should extend over several months if a true picture of a department's work is to be obtained. Such considerations are particularly important when a project report makes recommendations on future staffing. If a department's work is cyclical, the study must discover this fact and also the frequency and size of peak loading. An office supervisor NEBSS student, for example, could commence with a run of activity sampling readings towards the end of his first college term and continue these from time to time in the early new year.

Time study is not necessarily difficult in administrative areas but the observer needs to be very careful that he arrives at a fair, meaningful and negotiable work standard.

8.4 Time study

Typing work is suitable for the application of time study and incentive schemes, because it is repetitive and occupies large portions of total office time. The work study procedure and activity sampling have been described in detail at other chapters and we shall now proceed to look at a particular problem, the typing of orders for supplies to an organization.

Elemental breakdown. After discovering, through activity sampling, that order typing was a significant activity, it was then necessary to identify the elements in the task. These elements were listed, as shown in Figure 8.1. The purchase order consisted of a three-part order set, requiring the insertion of two pieces of carbon paper. Figure 8.1 shows a particular order (one of many timed) and it contains ten items.

Standard time. Before a standard time could be arrived at, it was necessary to know, with considerable accuracy, the size of an average order. Since this was such an important statistic, to be used in conjunction with the time study, it was decided to use a calculating machine to handle statistics obtained from one thousand orders on the files. The size of an average order was thus established as 4.38 items per order: if the typist produced one hundred orders, there would be 438 items typed. Using the same procedure, the average number of delivery date headings was found to be 1.23 per order.

Operation
Insert 2 carbons, break order set from pad.
To typewriter, insert and adjust set, move carriage and set.
Type firm and date.
Carriage, type delivery date, underline, carriage to first item.
Type item 1 and carriage return.
Type item 2.
Type item 3.
Type item 4.
Carriage, type delivery date, underline, carriage to next item.
Type item 5.
Type item 6.
Type item 7.
Carriage, type delivery date, underline, carriage to next item.
Type item 8.
Type item 9.
Type item 10.
Remove from typewriter, break set, place set to left and carbons to centre.

Note: A 3-part order set.

Figure 8.1 Elemental breakdown: order typing procedure for time study

The procedure for arriving at the work content for the elements of work in this job is shown at Figure 8.2. It only remained to use this information in order to build a standard time. Figure 8.3 shows how this was done, making allowances for

1. Average number of items per order
2. Average number of 'delivery date' headings per order
3. Work contingency allowances for 'legitimate fumbling'
4. Work contingency allowance for 'legitimate error correction' (erase and re-type)

The order-typing task studied here concerned very simple orders and the standard time of 1.372 minutes reflects this. If the order-typist clocks thirty-five working hours in a week, excluding any set tea breaks, then the company could expect her to produce 1530 orders in a week at standard performance. For this, an extra payment of perhaps one-third would be made. Thus a woman normally paid £18.00 per week under non-incentive conditions could earn £24.00 per week under the new scheme if she worked at standard performance. If a piece work system of payment is required, the piece work rate can be expressed as

$$\frac{2400}{1530} = 1.57 \text{ new pence per order typed}$$

Clerical work measurement

Element	Basic minutes (motivated)	Plus 14% rest and contingency	Special handling allowances	Work content
1. Insert 2 carbons, break order set from pad	0.17	0.194		0.194
2. To typewriter, insert and adjust, move carriage	0.09	0.103	From observation, one 'fumble' is allowed per 3 order sets (=0.05 mins. per set)	0.153
3. Type firm and date	0.13	0.148		0.148
4. Carriage, type delivery date, underline, carriage	0.15	0.171		0.171
5. Type item and carriage return	0.06	0.068		0.068
6. Remove set from typewriter, place to left, carbons to centre	0.11	0.125	From observation, one 'fumble' is allowed per 5 order sets (=0.024 mins. per set)	0.149

Figure 8.2 Summary of work content for the elements of work in order typing

Element	Calculations	Standard time (mins.)
1. Insert		0.194
2. To typewriter		0.153
3. Firm and date		0.148
4. Delivery date	1.23 × 0.171	0.210
5. Type items	4.38 × 0.068	0.298
6. Remove		0.149
	Time (per average order) (minutes)	1.152
Plus:		
Error correction allowance	13 seconds per average order (timed)	0.220
	Standard time per order	1.372

Note: Average items/order = 4.38.
Average date headings/order = 1.23.

Figure 8.3 Final make-up of standard time for order typing

Control statement. Figure 8.4 shows a simplified control statement for an order-typing section. It can be seen that although the typists are quite efficient when they are actually typing, the section output efficiency is only ninety-five per cent, due to absenteeism. The expected output (allowing for a budgeted five hours each week for filing duties) is arrived at as follows:

$$(3 \times 1530) - \left(5 \times \frac{1530}{35}\right) = 4371 \text{ expected orders typed (at standard) (approximately)}$$

$$\text{output efficiency} = \frac{4154}{4371} \times 100$$

$$= 95 \text{ per cent}$$

In practice the supervisor would be expected to make up the deficiency of 217 orders either by encouraging a higher productivity from the typists, arranging for overtime working or contributing herself by typing some (or some more) orders.

8.5 Systems

There are a large number of systems in use for the measurement of office work, which can be grouped in the following way:
1. Systems based on straightforward time study observations.
2. Systems based on predetermined motion times (PMTS).
3. Some form of estimating or synthesis. (Estimating is a means of assessing the time required to complete work, based on similar types of work, without using a detailed breakdown of the work into elements and their corresponding times at a defined level of performance. Synthesis is a technique for constructing the time for a task or part of a task at a defined level of performance, by adding the element times obtained previously from time studies on other tasks containing the same elements, or from data of a synthetic nature.)
4. Systems using rated activity sampling.

The first two groups are the recommended and most accurate methods, although good results could be obtained using 3: we shall now pay closer attention to number 2.

PMTS. The British Standards Institution has defined a predetermined motion time system as 'a work measurement technique whereby times established for basic human motions (classified according to the nature of the motion and the conditions under which it is made) are used to build up the time for a job at a defined level of performance'. A number of such systems, based mainly on elementary movements of the *Therblig* type, have gained increasing acceptance. These systems are often based on a large number of studies of individual movements, obtained by frame-by-frame

| Department: | Ordering | Section: | Order typing |

Week ending: ....

Typist	Total clocked hours	Standard production quantity	Actual production quantity	Production performance variance	Other duties Hrs.	Other duties Comments	General comments
A. Smith	35	1530	1630	+100	—		1 hour each day
B. Jones	30	1311	1200	−111	5	Filing	Absent one day
S. Mills	28	1224	1324	+100	—		
	93	4065	4154	+ 89			
		Target	4371				
		Output loss	217				
						Output efficiency 95 per cent	

Figure 8.4 Control statement for order typing

analysis of films taken over a range of operators performing a variety of tasks. Therblig is 'the name given by F. B. Gilbreth to each of the specific divisions of movement, according to the purpose for which it is made. These therbligs cover movements or reasons for the absence of movement. Each therblig has a specific colour, symbol and letter for recording purposes' (British Standard 3138: 1969). Three examples of therbligs are

⌒⊃ = search
⌒ = grasp
⌣ = transport (empty)

PMTS systems offer three main advantages:
1. They force people to give very close attention to work methods.
2. They allow accurate estimating to be carried out before the work is actually done. This can be very useful when planning facilities long in advance and when tendering for new business.
3. They lend themselves to computerization.

PMTS systems can be applied in varying degrees of detail (and therefore accuracy) to meet the needs of a situation. One system denotes these as 'detailed', 'simplified', and 'abbreviated'.

There are far too many PMTS systems to even attempt to cover in a general O and M book: Figure 8.5 gives some idea of the growth of knowledge in this field. The decision of which system to use must be based on the circumstances of the situation to be examined, but it is worth remembering that, as with activity sampling, in considering the difference between a detailed or simplified system, the purchaser gets the accuracy he pays for.

System	Origin
MTM	Methods Engineering Council, Pittsburgh (USA) 1948
MTM2	International MTM Directorate (1965)
PMTS	ICI Ltd. (derived from MTM)
SPMTS	ICI Ltd. 1959 (derived from PMTS)
Work factor	Work Factor Co. (Quick and Shea) 1938
BMT	Woods and Gordon Ltd. (Toronto) 1950 Presgrave and Bailey
Basic work data	ICI Ltd. (based on SPMTS)—for maintenance work
Master standard data	Serge A. Birn Co.
Universal standard data	H. B. Maynard Co. } MTM second-generation
Primary standard data	Urwick Orr
General purpose data	US MTM Association 1962

Figure 8.5 Some established PMTS systems

Taking a closer look at one of the systems, the simplified predetermined motion time system (SPMTS) developed by ICI Ltd. and introduced in 1959, we see that motions are divided into nine categories:
1. Motions of the trunk and legs
2. Reach and move
3. Grasp and release

Clerical work measurement

4. Turn
5. Crank
6. Apply pressure
7. Align
8. Eye and head motions
9. Combined and simultaneous motions

The initial training period for practitioners of SPMTS is quoted as rather less than one half of that which is required for the detailed technique, from which it was developed. As far as actual application time is concerned (that is, the time to complete a study), savings are in the region of twenty to thirty per cent.

Figure 8.6 is a typical (detailed) PMTS element description for a clerical procedure, omitting the derivation and codings for the time allowance against each element. These vary according to the chosen system and a training course is essential before a person can undertake PMTS analysis.

Element number	Element description	Time (minutes)
1	Reach to ball pen	
2	Grasp ball pen	
3	Move ball pen to form	
4	Position ball pen on form surface	
5	Make first stroke of an X	
6	Position for second stroke of X	
7	Make second stroke of the X	
8	Move ball pen to pen rack	
9	Align ball pen to pen rack	
10	Insert ball pen in pen rack	
11	Release ball pen	
12	Move hand to writing area	

Figure 8.6 Typical (detailed) PMTS element description for a clerical procedure

Examination questions

1. Describe how to establish standard times for work done in a general typing pool.
   (IWSP Graduate *Work Measurement*, 1969)
2. A standard time is in dispute and you have been asked to investigate. What steps would you take?
   (IWSP Graduate *Work Measurement*, 1969)
3. Establish the significant difference between
   (i) time study
   (ii) estimating
   (iii) analytical estimating
   (iv) synthesis
   (IWSP Graduate *Work Measurement*, 1969)

4. Define time study and explain some of its uses in O and M.
(HND Business Studies)
5. Differentiate between synthesis and time study and state what you consider to be the advantages of the former over the latter. Explain the applications of synthesis in the initial design of a manufacturing plant.
(IWM *Management Techniques*)
6. Describe two method study techniques that could be used for an initial investigation of activity within a typing pool of 20 to 30 girls.
(IWSP *Method Study—Technical and Clerical*, 1974)
7. (i) Explain the likely causes of excessive walking in an office.
    (ii) Describe how the overall effectiveness of the staff could be improved in this situation.
(IWSP *Method Study—Technical and Clerical*, 1972)
8. (i) Why is it necessary to undertake interviewing as part of a clerical work study assignment?
    (ii) What means should be adopted to ensure an effective interview?
(IWSP *Method Study—Technical and Clerical*, 1973)
9. Describe, with reasons, six aspects that should be considered when investigating efficiency in an office.
(IWSP *Associated Techniques A*, 1974)
10. (i) Describe the preliminary steps to be taken before the application of clerical work measurement.
    (ii) Outline those managerial and office staff attitudes that might need to be changed to ensure co-operation.
(IWSP *Work Measurement—Technical and Clerical*, 1974)
11. Discuss the suitability of each of the following techniques for measuring clerical work:
    (i) time study
    (ii) synthesis
    (iii) analytical estimating
    (iv) activity sampling
(IWSP *Work Measurement—Technical and Clerical*, 1974)
12. (i) Describe the procedure to be followed in using work measurement techniques in an office.
    (ii) Show how the resultant data from using work measurement can be used.
(IWSP *Work Measurement—Technical and Clerical*, 1972)
13. Explain fully what is meant by each of the following times:
    (i) allowed   (iv) attendance   (vii) idle
    (ii) standard   (v) attention   (viii) observed
    (iii) basic   (vi) waiting   (ix) elapsed
(IWSP *Work Measurement—Technical and Clerical*, 1972)
14. Describe the fatigue factors that are most likely to be encountered when assessing relaxation allowances for clerical work.
(IWSP *Work Measurement—Technical and Clerical*, 1973)

9
Specialist O and M techniques

9.1 Systems analysis

Most supervisors will be familiar with the word system in their business and social lives. For example, a betting system refers to an ordered or methodical procedure for placing bets, with the aim of increasing one's chances of winning. The dictionary uses a number of words to describe the meaning of system and the following general picture emerges: 'a system involves the use of distinct method, logically or scientifically based, to arrange human activities in regular, methodical order'.

In Chapter 1 (Section 1.6, page 10) we discussed the management services concept and Figure 1.4 illustrated the structure of a management services department in a sizeable company. Four main sections of this service department were shown:
1. Administration and secretarial
2. O and M
3. Computers: (i) Programming
    (ii) Systems analysis
    (iii) Operating and data preparation
4. Operational research (OR)

Systems analysis was used here in the sense of putting an information system on to a computer, although we shall see shortly that this is a conveniently restricted use of the phrase. In the same discussion, readers should note that O and M has a role which includes providing assistance to the systems analyst by providing whatever back-up service may be required in terms of already-available information on a particular department's organization and methods.

Definition. Systems analysis may be theoretically defined as 'a scientific process or method of approach to the achievement of desired objectives in human affairs. It involves a systematic examination and comparative study of the alternative actions open to those wishing to achieve the desired objectives. It involves a comparison of the alternative courses of action often using conceptual models to predict performance, based on such factors as the cost of required resources (resource cost) and the associated benefits expected from each alternative course of action. Fundamental to the whole concept of general systems analysis is the formal consideration of uncertainty in business decision-making, with the object of reducing the risk of uncertainty.'

As mentioned above and at Chapter 1, systems analysis has been conveniently considered (in the management services concept) as concerned with putting an information system on to a computer. Repetition at this point is quite intentional, since the idea of management information systems is fundamental to the aims of management services work.

Management information systems. In an earlier chapter we saw that a company organization structure may be considered to be a communications network, through which the management decision-making process works and objectives are achieved.

Some supervisors may not yet be aware of the complications in office procedures and the related paperwork: particularly those supervisors newly appointed to office supervision and the shop floor. Supervisors undertaking courses of study involving the completion of a work study of some management system will, of course, gain first-hand experience of such complications (for example NEBSS, IWSP, IWM or City & Guilds Work Study certificates and diplomas).

To some supervisors, placing an order is a straightforward business, merely requiring a request to be made. In practice, there can be very many complications, especially if there are:
1. A large quantity of orders to be placed
2. A wide range of items to be ordered
3. Associated purchasing decisions, such as supplier-suitability, quantity discounts and short lead-times
4. Internal and external communications problems of keeping records of orders and goods received

Figure 9.1 attempts to show the information flow in the purchasing procedure for a medium-sized engineering company. This is just one of very many procedures in a factory and readers will note that a number of other departments are involved in a purchase order being placed, right from the start. The systems analyst is vitally concerned with information flow and the design of accurate and minimal-waste communication systems.

Systems study and design. These may be considered as the hard-core result of applying systems analysis thinking. The object clearly is to design effective new systems or more effective systems than those already in existence. Systems study follows the work study principles already discussed in other chapters and should always challenge the need for a particular procedure before trying to streamline or integrate it. Basic questions in the case quoted above would therefore be
1. Do we need to purchase materials?
2. Do we need a purchase-order procedure?

Systems analysts, when investigating existing systems and seeking new

Specialist O and M techniques

(or better) systems, will generally follow the following basic procedure:
1. Define the real problem
2. Identify or select true objectives
3. Identify and unite the various systems
4. Analyze these systems
5. Choose the best alternatives, bearing in mind the cost of required resources and the expected associated benefits
6. Plan for efficient and effective implementation (action)

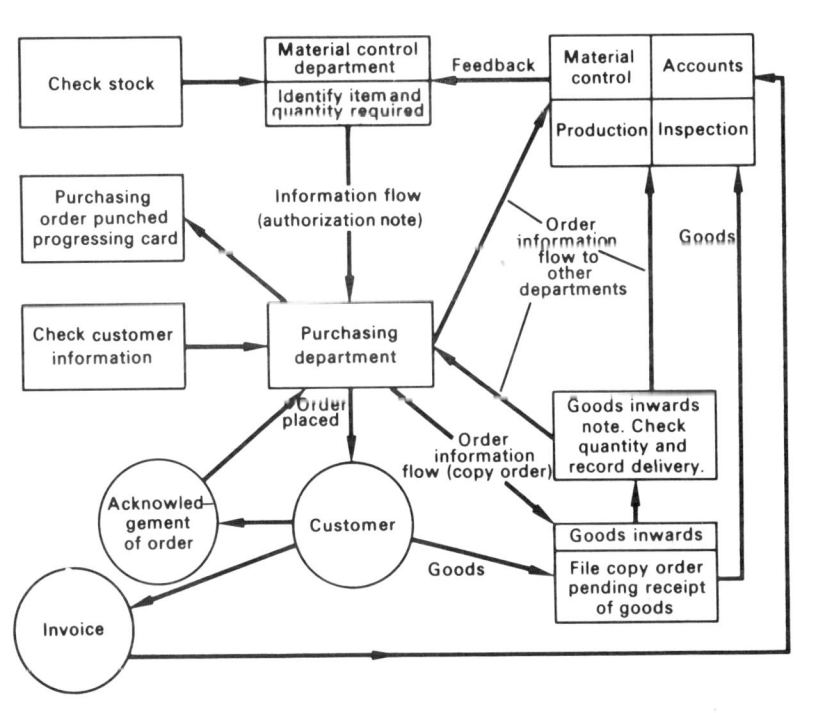

Figure 9.1 Example of information flow in a purchasing procedure (engineering company)

Check list. A systems analysis check list for a purchasing department such as the one quoted earlier (and in Chapter 10) could be as follows. This should give supervisors an idea of the scope of such investigations:
1. Plans and objectives
2. Organization structure
3. Policies
4. Systems and procedures
5. Personnel implications

6. Layout and equipment
7. Operation and control methods.

In order to help readers to understand what is required of the systems analyst, Figure 9.2 shows an extract from a college systems analysis course. It will be noted that at Stage 10 (in Figure 9.2), the words input and output are used: a short explanatory note is necessary here. *Input* is the part of the systems analyst's work that involves capturing the necessary data and presenting it in a suitable form for feeding into a computer. There is a clear and obvious link here between the work of the systems analyst and the O and M officer in designing sound clerical procedures. Typical questions on the systems analyst's check sheet are

Stage	Aspect
1	Introduction to systems analysis
2	Elements of systems analysis
3	Outline of different stages
4	Investigation techniques
5	Introduction to punched card equipment
6	Practical examples
7	Introduction to documentation techniques
8	Documentation in detail
9	Introduction to the analysis stage
10	Input/output/forms and documentation systems analysis stage
11	Flow charting and O and M techniques
12	Principles of systems design
13	Decision tables

Figure 9.2 Outline of a college systems analysis course

1. What clerical skills are required in producing satisfactory input?
2. What data capturing and preparation speeds are required by the computer?

Form design will clearly play an important part in the input stage. The systems analyst will have less problems with *output* than with input where people are often involved in data preparation. Nevertheless, he must be careful to design the output so as to be of maximum use to users. Many supervisors will have seen the most common form of output from business computers, in the form of high speed line printers, often using pre-printed stationery (again a case for sound form design).

9.2 Operational research

Definition. Operational research is comprehensively defined as 'the application of the methods of science to complex problems arising in the direction and management of large systems of men, machines, materials and money in industry, business, government and defence. The distinctive approach is to develop a scientific model of the system,

Specialist O and M techniques

incorporating measurements of factors such as chance and risk, with which to predict and compare the outcomes of alternative decisions, strategies or controls. The purpose is to help management determine its policy and action scientifically.' (British Standard 3138: 1969.)

Optimization. The overall aim of operational research is to discover the necessary management decisions in the best interests of the whole organization (optimization). A good example is the inventory policy of a manufacturing company. (The word inventory implies raw material stocks, work-in-progress and finished goods stocks.) This is an executive-type problem. Let us briefly consider the basic attitudes of four major departments of the factory towards the inventory policy.

The *production* director will tend to prefer long, uninterrupted runs, with the associated reduced set-up and tooling costs. Unfortunately, such long runs could result in a larger inventory than necessary and also fewer product lines to offer the marketing organization (and consequently the customers). One of the *finance* director's main objectives is to reduce inventory, as this may be a very high figure in some manufacturing companies (perhaps a quarter of the annual sales figure). Such money tends to be tied up permanently and the finance director seeks to reduce such capital investment. The *marketing* director is intent on offering customers and potential customers immediate or quick delivery over a wide range of the company's products. Ideally, he would also like to see the production department able to make special and short-notice orders. The *personnel* director is intent on achieving a stabilized work force, with the company offering consistent overtime working and minimum redundancies. This can often be achieved, for example, by producing goods for inventory during slack sales periods.

All this may seem to suggest that the idea of a management team is a myth, bearing in mind the major conflicts possible from the above considerations. It is, indeed, a major part of the operational research worker's job to put down guidelines for a sensible spread and balance of overall management effort. In the above situation, the operational research worker aims to arrive at the best inventory policy for the whole organization.

OR techniques. As operational research covers the whole range of management decision-making, its techniques are many but they fall naturally into main areas, some of which are outlined below.

1. *Stock control* is concerned with the logic of replenishment. Typical aims include the determination of economic purchasing or manufacturing quantities and the necessary safety stocks to be carried.

2. *Replacement* is necessary because all systems deteriorate with the passage of time and corrective action must be taken. Some systems, for example light bulbs, fail completely: that is to say, they are either useful or totally useless. It is one thing to replace light bulbs in a private house, but what policy should be adopted for a large city? This would be a

problem for the operational research worker and maintenance policies in general fall in this field of study. The theory of probability is applied.

3. *Probability* deals with uncertainty in business problems of all kinds. These range from the expected incidence of machine breakdowns to sales forecasts and transport arrival times. Statistical techniques are used.

4. *Forecasting* is a technique which attempts to forecast future demands for products or services and assists higher management to make, for example, wise investment decisions and production plans. Statistical analysis is used a great deal in this area.

5. *Queueing theory* often uses models of systems to enable a prediction to be made of how the system would respond to demands made on it. Operational research workers and O and M officers have used this technique to analyze such problems as counter-manning in post offices and supermarkets, and equipment requirements for centralized dictation systems in offices. All these problems have a common base: the maximum number of 'customers' to be satisfied by the minimum number of service points. Customers can be ships or lorries docking, as well as people.

6. *Project network analysis* is defined (in British Standard 4335: 1972) as 'a group of techniques for presenting the description, analysis, planning and control of projects which consider the logical inter-relationships of all project activities. The group includes techniques concerned with time, resources, costs and other influencing factors, e.g. uncertainty.' Well-known techniques of project network analysis include critical path analysis (CPA) and programme evaluation review technique (PERT).

7. *Linear programming:* this is one of the techniques of mathematical programming, aimed at utilizing limited resources to the best advantage. Objectives of linear programming might be the minimizing of cost or maximizing of profit. Graphical methods can be used to solve the simpler problems where there are not too many variables.

8. *Theory of games* involves the use of carefully designed games to simulate business problems. The aim is to test alternative strategies, often using computer facilities, so as to arrive at the best strategy for the organization concerned.

9. *Dynamic programming* is a technique with similar aims to those of linear programming, but it is not constrained by some of the assumptions necessary with that technique. Dynamic programming is useful, in particular, for problems involving decisions which are taken at distinct stages, such as every month.

OR examples. It is not possible to give examples here illustrating all of the above OR techniques. However, it will be useful to illustrate two of them, in order to give supervisors a clearer idea of the subject.

A queueing problem exists in centralized dictation installations, where a large number of people are given dictating points, linked with a bank of recording machines in a secretarial services department. The dictated

Specialist O and M techniques

letter, memo or report is recorded by some means, such as tape. One of the problems facing the O and M officer concerns the number of recording machines required.

Let us suppose that there are sixty people requiring to use the service. From a systems study, the O and M officer discovers that the demand is random and each dictator uses the service, on average, once a day for eleven minutes. The working day is 410 minutes. A service factor (S) is calculated, as follows:

$$S = \frac{\text{average servicing time }(t)}{t + \text{average idle time}}$$

$$= \frac{11}{11 + (410 - 11)}$$

$$= \frac{11}{410}$$

and $S = 0.027$

Reference can then be made to queueing tables against sixty people (known as the population) and the service factor, calculated above (0.027). Against these values can be read off the number of service points (N) (in this case, recording machines) and the statistical probability of a delay (p):

N	p
4	0.086
3	0.263
2	0.655

The interpretation of the above values of p is as follows:
1. With two recording machines ($N=2$), almost seven-tenths of the demands for access to a machine will meet with a delay (an unacceptable proportion).
2. With four recording machines ($N=4$), just less than one-tenth of the demands for access to a machine will meet with a delay (this could be considered quite acceptable in some organizations).

The tables also enable the average length of waiting time to be read off:

N	Average delay (minutes)
4	0.66
3	3.3
2	21.1

Assuming four machines, for example, then for every 1000 attempts to obtain access to a machine, this will *not* be possible immediately on only eighty-six occasions, when the actual waiting time will probably be in the region of 0.66 minutes (approximately forty seconds). This kind of information is very useful to management when making decisions on equipment purchasing.

We shall now look at an example of network analysis, more specifically using the critical path analysis (CPA) method, which is also sometimes referred to as critical path method (CPM). A network diagram is drawn to show work to be done (activities) and their relatedness with each other. A main feature of this technique of project network analysis is the calculation of the minimum total project duration, known as the critical path (that sequence of activities which dictates the total project duration).

Figure 9.3 shows a critical path network for the design and manufacture of a large gearbox consisting essentially of a cast housing and forged shafts and gears (all machined). The design stage is known as activity 1–2 and the circles denote distinct events in time: for example, the start and finish of design work. The significance of the relative positions of the various activities may be illustrated by reference to three activities (1–2, 2–3 and 2–7):

1. Neither order-placing (2–3) nor tool design (2–7) can proceed until the design stage (1–2) is completed.
2. Once design is completed, both 2–3 and 2–7 can proceed simultaneously.

Activity 4–8 is known as a dummy activity and there is actually no activity. The dummy indicates that the machining of castings (4–5) cannot proceed until the tools are available (7–8).

If readers trace the various paths through this network from left to right, one path will be found to have the longest duration:

1–2–3–8–9–10–6–12–13 (35.2 weeks)

Note that there is spare time in various paths of this network. These are known as float activities, the spare time being known as float time. For example, consider the section of the network 2–3–8–7. The critical path time is one week plus eighteen weeks, making nineteen weeks (path 2–3–8): the alternative path (2–7–8) totals four weeks plus four weeks, making eight weeks. The float time is therefore:

19 weeks − 8 weeks = 11 weeks.

It is important to note that any delay on any critical path activity will result in the whole project being late. This does not apply to float activities. As we have seen, we have eleven weeks to play with at the tool design and tool manufacture stages.

One big advantage of this technique is that manpower and equipment can be moved from one project to another, providing there is flexibility of these facilities.

Before we leave this example, let us consider a problem.

One way of shortening the critical path time of the network shown is to release drawings into production at different stages of design. Suppose that the design can be subdivided into three stages and drawings can be released early, as follows:

1. After four weeks release casting and forging drawings.

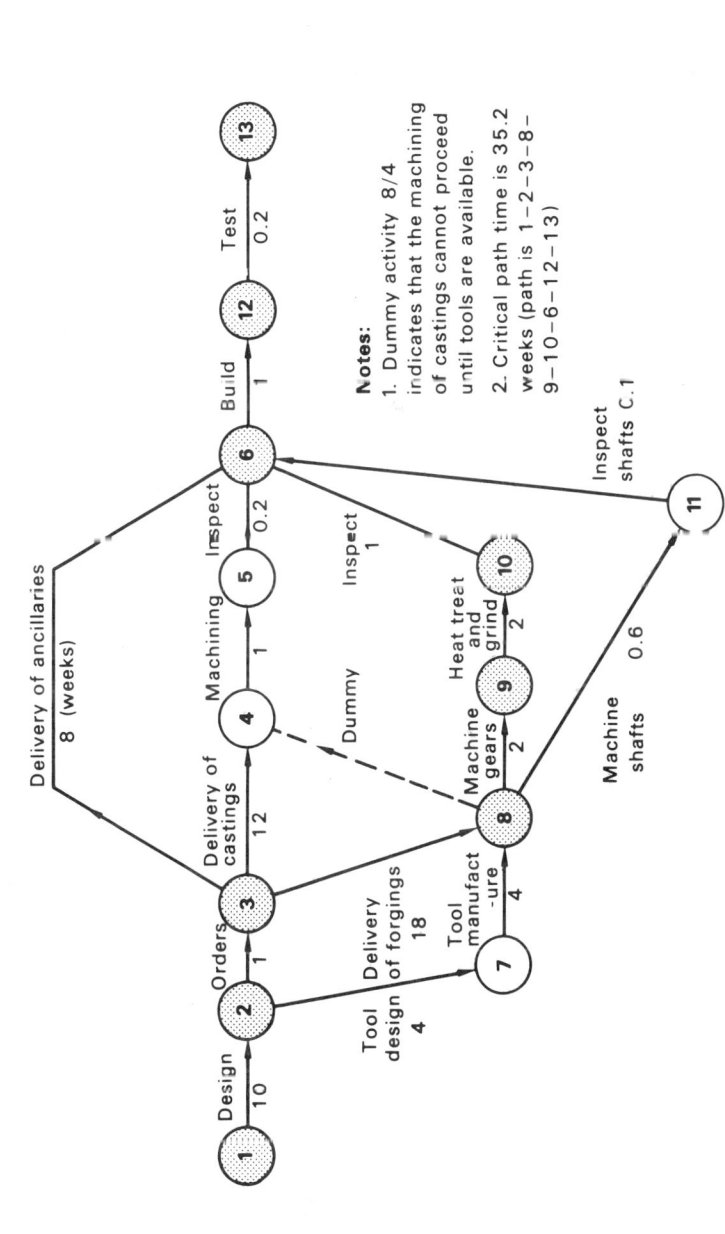

Figure 9.3 Critical path network for the design and manufacture of a large gearbox

Notes:
1. Dummy activity 8/4 indicates that the machining of castings cannot proceed until tools are available.
2. Critical path time is 35.2 weeks (path is 1–2–3–8–9–10–6–12–13)

2. After a further three weeks release information for tooling to be designed and manufactured.

It is possible, in this way, to secure a reduction in critical path time of at least seven weeks. Redraw the network to prove that this significant improvement can be achieved.

Figure 9.4 illustrates an extract from a typical computer print-out for a building project. In this PERT example, the events are printed in order of increasing 'slack' (or float). If the information is presented in this way, it is referred to as a slack order print-out. Other kinds of print-out are expected order date, latest order date and even order number. In practice, it is very useful for the performance data to be presented under departmental headings, in order that the managers concerned may only receive lists of activities for which they are responsible.

O and M and computers. The management services concept has been outlined in Chapter 1 and the four main sections of this service department were shown and repeated at the beginning of this chapter.

When systems analysis is seen to be and operates as a separate function from O and M, the term O and M is then understood to mean the investigation of general work, over a wide range of activities. For example, office incentive schemes, general office machinery, training and development schemes and communications and organizational problems. As mentioned in Chapter 1, O and M would also be expected to provide valuable assistance to the systems analyst by providing whatever back-up service may be required in terms of already-available information on a particular department's organization and methods.

As well as the systems analyst, the operational research worker leans heavily on the computer and OR workers rely on masses of statistical information on company activities. Part of the O and M department's function is to provide such statistics, based on their actual experience and observation in the areas concerned.

It must be pointed out that only the larger organizations will have a management services department such as that shown at Figure 1.4 (page 11). It has been said that a company needs to employ over 2000 people before it can employ a full-time OR team. The management services department shown at Figure 1.4 could be typical of a progressive company employing in the region of 3000 upwards. In a progressive smaller company, there could simply be a small O and M team. In this case, the relationship between O and M and the computer is as follows (the computer may be on the company's premises or it may be in a service bureau):

1. Much of the systems analysis work will be undertaken by the O and M personnel, working closely with either the computer manufacturer's personnel or the computer service bureau's personnel.
2. The O and M personnel will be very closely involved in form design

PERT Programme (extract)

Starting event	Ending event	Activity	Duration (weeks)	Completion dates			Float (or slack)	Costs	
				Actual	Expected	Latest		Actual	Expected
20	28	D Steelwork	6	6 June 74	6 June 74	6 June 74	0	£450 OT	£400
10	16	M Concrete end pillars	4		12 June 74	24 July 74	6		£850

Note: D = Drawings.
OT = Unplanned overtime.
M = Manufacture.

Figure 9.4 Heading of a 'slack (float) order' computer printout for a building project: events printed in order of increasing slack

in order that data is 'captured' efficiently and management information disseminated.

Generally, whether in an organization using their own systems analysts or otherwise, O and M practitioners are expected to identify areas for computerization. The nature of O and M work, intimately involved as it is with a wide range of company activities, makes it an ideal vehicle for unearthing suitable computer applications.

Figure 9.5 shows the method study process chart summary table from an O and M investigation of a supplies ordering procedure in a local

Location	○	▽	□	◁	D	
Stage 1: raising requisition to order being mailed Operational depot Administrative headquarters	4 7	1 2	1 3	3 7	0 0	
Stage 2: receipt of copy order, goods and delivery note, to goods received note being sent to administrative HQ (from depot) Operational depot	10	7	3	13	0	
Stage 3: at administrative HQ from receiving statement, invoice, goods received notes, to paying accounts Administrative headquarters (a) Typing section (b) General office	7 12	2 8	1 4	6 16	0 0	
Stage 4: other procedures (involving the stores requisition clerk) Administrative headquarters	3	1	2	8	0	
						GRAND TOTAL
TOTALS	43	21	14	53	0	131

Figure 9.5 Summary table from an O and M investigation of a supplies ordering procedure in a local government organization

government organization. A brief examination shows the complexity of the clerical operations involved in what should be the fairly simple process. Forty-three operations were involved as well as fifty-three transports, contributing ninety-six to the total of 131 activities. When such complexity is discovered by O and M practitioners in repetitive

Specialist O and M techniques

work, it is not unusual for a change to computer processing to be recommended. In this case, the O and M report recommended that the weekly ordering of the bulk of supplies be discontinued and replaced by standing orders. This was to be regarded as an interim step preceding the computerization of the whole procedure when the authority's computer was delivered in three years' time.

Systems analysis requires its own flow charting technique which is somewhat similar to the method study flow charting procedure discussed in detail in this book. Readers wishing to make reference to the terminology and symbols may refer to British Standards 3527 and 4058.

Commercial applications of computers start in feasibility study and systems study. An important part of the feasibility study is often done by the O and M practitioner as mentioned earlier, through his knowledge and collected data on company operations. Activity sampling is also a very useful tool in the hands of O and M practitioners, supplying very useful information in computer feasibility studies such as:

1. What activities are taking place.
2. Which of these are suitable for computer handling.
3. What time-saving there would be if the work was loaded on to a computer.

Once the systems analysis stage has been passed and the programming stage reached, the influence of O and M ceases. There is then no question of whether a procedure is necessary or whether there could be a better way of achieving the objectives. The charting then takes the form of machine instructions, frequently concerned with decision stages. For example, in a computerized payroll application, if the effective total taxable pay is not greater than (say) £600, no tax calculations are necessary. However, if it is greater than £600, the computer will calculate

$$(T-600) \times \frac{7}{9} \text{ and so on,}$$

arriving at the total tax due (multipliers and other standards will depend on the taxation system in use at the time).

Examination questions

1. What relationship does O and M have with OR?
   (Part of HND Business Studies question)
2. What do you understand by critical path analysis? Set out the objectives and basic essentials of this technique and explain its relationship with work study.
   (IWSP Graduate *Method Study*, 1969)
3. What problems may arise in establishing OR in an organization?
   (IWSP Graduate *Associated Techniques*, 1969)

4. Discuss the need for a computer and the contribution it can make in critical path analysis work.
(IWSP Graduate *Associated Techniques*, 1969)
5. What do you understand by the expression operational research? Discuss the relationship with work study.
(IWSP Graduate *Method Study*, 1969)
6. Explain in general terms how OR techniques can help in any two of the following:
    (i) inventory control
    (ii) allocation of resources
    (iii) queueing problems
(IWSP Graduate *Associated Techniques*, 1968)
7. (i) Define OR and discuss an area of application in either a commercial or manufacturing organization.
    (ii) Discuss an optimization problem which could exist between the sales, finance and production functions of a manufacturing company.
    (iii) What relationship does O and M have with OR?
(HND Business Studies)
8. (i) What are the conventions used in preparing a critical path network?
    (ii) Draw a simple network to illustrate these conventions.
    (iii) Explain how the critical path for a network is determined.
(IWSP *Associated Techniques*, 1973)
9. Discuss the uses of queueing theory.
(IWSP *Associated Techniques B*, 1974)
10. (i) What are the objectives of project network analysis?
    (ii) Demonstrate by means of a simple diagram how these objectives can be achieved.
    (iii) What is understood by float?
(IWSP *Associated Techniques B*, 1974)
11. (i) What is the purpose of operational research?
    (ii) Why is it becoming increasingly important to management?
    (iii) Describe briefly how operational research can assist in plant replacement decisions.
(IWSP *Associated Techniques B*, 1974)
12. Discuss, with a suitable example, critical path analysis as the basis for project control.
(IWSP *Associated Techniques B*, 1974)
13. (i) Why is activity sampling often used in the study of office work?
    (ii) The following data were obtained from a pilot study in a typing pool:
    60 per cent of time spent on clerical work
    25 per cent of time spent in taking dictation
    15 per cent of time spent on typing

Calculate for each activity the number of observations required to give 95 per cent limit of accuracy, at a 95 per cent confidence level.

(IWSP *Work Measurement—Technical and Clerical*, 1972)

14. (i) Describe the technique of activity sampling.
    (ii) What are its main uses?
    (iii) An activity was estimated to occupy 25 per cent of the study period. Calculate the number of observations required to confirm this estimate within ±5 per cent at 95 per cent confidence limits.

(IWSP *Work Measurement—Technical and Clerical*, 1974)

15. Using the information in Table 9.1, complete the following:
    (i) Draw the network and state the earliest completion time.
    (ii) State the sub-critical path.
    (iii) What would be the effect of activity F being three days late?

(IWSP *Associated Techniques B*, 1973)

Activity	Dependent activities	Duration (days)
A	lead activity	4
B	A	5
C	B	12
D	A	5
E	D	8
F	C	10
G	A	4
H	G	2
J	H	9
K	J	7
M	C, F, K, L	3
N	M	2
L	A	25

Table 9.1

16. (i) State very briefly what is understood by method study and systems analysis.
    (ii) Describe their similarities and differences.

(IWSP *Associated Techniques A*, 1972)

17. Discuss the application of network analysis techniques in industry. Your answer should show your understanding of the mechanics of such techniques.

(Institution of Works Managers college paper)

18. Explain in simple terms what is meant by critical path analysis.

(NEBSS Certificate, 1971)

10
General aspects of O and M

10.1 Report writing

Bearing in mind the general subject matter of this book, we are not concerned here with merely reporting on such aspects as safety and performance. The type of report we are considering is a form of communication in a company organization, providing positive feedback of recommendations from the writer to his management in order that new, soundly-based decisions may be made. The term positive feedback may be regarded as management jargon, but it offers a useful analogy with machine control systems where actual performance is automatically fed back into a control unit, for correction, repetition or planned changes. In our case, the positive feedback means the return to management of useful information.

An organization is a complex network of communications which should bind the organization together into an efficient working group. It follows that a management report which causes confusion, dissension or strife is not making an effective contribution. Unfortunately, very few people have the natural ability to communicate well in writing without receiving education and training in the subject. The modern supervisor is positioned at a strategic point in his organization's communications or information transmission network. It is very important for him to project or superimpose his personality on to this network.

Verboseness. As modern business affairs tend to be complicated, and the problems wide-ranging, it is perhaps not surprising that people have a tendency to produce long memoranda, reports, letters, telex and teleprinter messages. Such people are often under the impression that a complex situation demands a complex piece of writing. However, such situations may often demand quite the opposite treatment.

Objective. The prime objective of efficient written communication must be to increase the amount of intelligent co-operation between different areas of the organization. The communications technique used must match in quality the science and technology of the particular industry or

General aspects of O and M 145

business concerned. In this chapter we are really considering the supervisor's personal projection, through written media, into the area of management decision-making.

Origination significance. A well-constructed report from a supervisor is important for a number of reasons:

1. It provides useful first-hand information to senior management, so that new, soundly-based management decisions may be made.
2. It can provide a useful base document to be subsequently used by other company professionals, such as work study officers, accountants, operational research officers, and O and M officers, as a springboard for more thorough and wider-ranging investigations.
3. It can stand in its own right as a first hand, 'on the spot' comment or record of shop floor (or office floor) activities.
4. The written report is an important discipline in itself and requires the supervisor to commit himself to a permanently-recorded statement of fact or opinion.
5. Facts must be presented, and in many cases some analysis of the facts, in order to draw or suggest conclusions. The report can therefore draw attention to important matters and include others into the exercise.
6. In some cases a written report commits to paper, for the first time, some vital information that is perhaps carried in someone's head or on scraps of paper in a desk or notebook.

Study project. The aim of a study project, leading to a management report, should be to achieve one or more of the following objectives: a direct (measurable) cost saving; increased efficiency (using an agreed interpretation of this expression); improved working conditions. The second of these includes those projects that clearly improve the efficiency of a service to management, but the improved efficiency may be difficult to measure in terms of money saved. However, increased efficiency may be very clearly evident, for example, in the reduction of time delays between procedures. The third of the objectives includes those projects that clearly improve the working environment in such a way as to create a more contented labour force. This may be done, for example, by introducing better work place layouts, equipment and general facilities. Direct cost savings may then result from reduced labour turnover and increased productivity. However, such benefits may again be difficult to measure in terms of direct cost savings.

The wise supervisor will always consider the personal outworkings of his technical reports, particularly in manufacturing organizations.

Guide points. There is no single, correct way to write a management report, because of the wide variety of management situations and the differences between individual companies or businesses. However, senior management will expect a certain standard of presentation, although they are unlikely to be obsessively pedantic unless they work for a government-type organization.

The following points should be considered by supervisors wishing to achieve the maximum acceptance of their reports:

1. Senior management will not be impressed if they are required to spend a long time wading through a complex, jumbled report, before they can discover what the writer means.
2. They will expect to see a summary of recommendations and justifiable cost savings, where these are claimed.
3. They will expect to be able easily to assimilate the present method and proposed method where a report is of the method-improvement type.
4. They will expect to be able easily to find in the report that information which unquestionably supports any recommendations made or conclusions drawn.
5. They will not be impressed with the physical size of the report.
6. They will not be impressed with a writer who is unable to give clear answers to questions concerning the report.
7. They will not be impressed with jargon.

Principles. Management reports fall into three main types:

1. The general type of report, dealing with major aspects. This may break completely new ground: for example, a company may not have any arrangements at all for introducing and training new recruits and the report may suggest a definite induction and training programme that could have far-reaching effects.
2. The technical or method improvement types of report, using a range of management techniques such as management accountancy, work study and operational research. These reports have a definite, measurable, 'before-and-after' basis and the O and M report falls into this category.
3. The technical type of report dealing with a wide range of individual day-to-day matters requiring financial or general advice.

General type reports are probably best presented in the following form:

The subject of the report
An introduction
The findings of the report
Any conclusions drawn from the report
Any recommendations based on the findings
Necessary references
A summary

This is usually known as an inductive approach (starting with an introduction, with the recommendations following) compared with a deductive approach (presenting the recommendations first).

The technical or method improvement type of report naturally

General aspects of O and M

requires the marshalling and presentation of a large amount of technical information, statistics and descriptive matter. In some smaller companies, the supervisor may find it necessary to do the job of the O and M officer or work study officer in his own area until the company is large enough to employ a full-time specialist, or hire a management consultant. The same basic ideas can then be followed for his report as for the general type report, but a special (and more detailed) format may be necessary. Listed below are the essential points in its presentation.

The O and M Report
1. Title page
2. Contents
3. Terms of reference
4. Summary report form for main recommendations (see Figure 10.1)
5. Summary recommendations
6. Aim of study
7. Introduction
8. Description of present method (personnel and equipment)
9. Comments on present method
10. Development of better method
11. Description of proposed method (personnel and equipment)
12. Comments on proposed method
13. Cost analysis (economic implications)
14. Appreciation (acknowledgements)
15. Bibliography

Appendix I   Information on present method, including full index
Appendix II Information on proposed method, including full index

The other type of technical report, possibly involving the supervisor, would normally be a much less complicated affair, ranging over a narrower field. Some sample subjects might be discussions of whether the company should rent some vending machines or whether the hours of work in the offices should be altered or staggered. The general advice in these cases is to keep the report as short and as free from jargon as possible.

10.2 Form design

Technical aspects. One of the most significant changes in the life of a newly-appointed supervisor is his involvement in paperwork through the handling of a large number of forms. It is a mistake to regard forms as rather useless or time-wasting encumbrances. In fact, the supervisor who handles forms carefully will be well-noted by management.

Forms have two basic purposes: the collection of information, through a permanent (written) record on the form provided and the

Summary Report				
Subject title:			Summary report no.: SR 64	
Authorized by:			Undertaken by:	
Date commenced:			Date completed:	
Agreed terms of reference:				
Main recommendations				
Recommendation	Financial		Personnel	
	Expected savings	Capital expenditure	Aspects	
1				
2				
3				
4				
5				
6				
Maintenance and other like costs:				
Proposed financial commitment				
Cash flow				
Quarter	1 2 3	4	1 2 3	4
Source of cash and repayment details:				
Signed:			Date:	

Figure 10.1 Summary O and M report

communication of that captured information to those needing it. On the last point, O and M officers are interested to discover what happens to copies generated and distributed from prime documents such as the works order. It may be that a certain department receives copies regularly but has no use for them, other than to put them on file. In such a case, the department does not need the copy form and should be removed from the circulation list.

General aspects of O and M 149

Design. It will not be surprising to supervisors to hear that forms, like any other management procedure, need to be carefully designed. Form design is another duty of the O and M officer and a newly-introduced system may fail or succeed depending upon the forms used.

Below is a list of reasons why real thinking needs to be applied to the design of forms for business use, from the twin standpoints of physical make-up and subsequent use:

1. The form must be an absolutely clear communication to the persons who are required to enter information on it. There must be no chance of errors due to misunderstanding.
2. Forms need to be designed carefully so as to avoid unnecessary printing and paper costs being incurred in their production.
3. Many forms need to be designed so as to work efficiently in conjunction with office machinery.
4. Many forms need to be designed in order to survive the rough passage through work-in-progress stages in manufacturing areas.

Figure 10.2 shows an extract from the newly-designed purchasing procedures for a medium size engineering company, after an O and M investigation revealed that the current procedures were inadequate. It can be seen that *form instructions* were built into the new procedures and eight new forms were designed. Three important features should be noted:

1. Each form carries a unique number.
2. These numbers and relevant details are recorded in a forms manual.
3. Each form has printed on it the correct paper or card size.

Let us take a closer look at item 1 in the figure, purchasing order 646–1–2 10 in. × 8¼ in. The form number in the forms manual is shown to be 646. The number following it indicates whether the form is a first or a subsequent issue: in this case, the 1 indicates a first issue (or design). The last number indicates whether the form is part of a multi-part set: in this case, the purchasing order is used in conjunction with another form at the order-typing stage, namely form 646A–1–2 (spirit-master sheet). The latter carries the same forms manual number except that it is followed by an A, signifying that this form is 'bred' from another and does not stand in its own right. To clarify this: the purchasing order was typed together with the purchasing order spirit master sheet (using spirit master paper between them). The master sheet was then used on a spirit duplicating machine to produce various copies for internal company use (for example, the goods inwards copy—Form 648–1–1). The purchasing order punched progressing card (651–1–1) was also passed through a spirit duplicating machine and readers will therefore appreciate the need for accurate specification and control of paper sizes.

It is hoped that supervisors will now be closer to an appreciation of the work that goes into form design and the importance of complying with any instructions relating to the supervisor's part in the process. This latter point will now be taken up separately.

The supervisor's contribution. We shall now sum up the points concerning the supervisor's contribution to the effective use of forms.

1. Supervisors must ensure that they fully understand the meaning of the forms used in their departments.
2. They must ensure that all their personnel receive instruction in this and appreciate the importance of careful paperwork processing.

	Purchasing procedures		
1.	Terms of reference		
2.	Principles		
3.	Procedures		
4.	Staffing		
	Form instructions		
		Form number	Size
1.	Purchasing order	646–1–2	10 in. × $8\frac{1}{4}$ in.
2.	Purchasing order (continuation)	647–1–2	10 in. × $8\frac{1}{4}$ in.
3.	Purchasing order spirit master sheet	646A–1–2	$8\frac{3}{4}$ in. × $8\frac{1}{4}$ in.
4.	Purchasing order (continuation) spirit master sheet	647A–1–2	$8\frac{3}{4}$ in. × $8\frac{1}{4}$ in.
5.	Goods inward copy (of purchasing order)	648–1–1	10 in. × $7\frac{1}{2}$ in.
6.	Purchase authorization	649–1–1	6 in. × 8 in.
7.	Goods inward note (interleaved carbon set)	650–1–2	8 in. × $8\frac{1}{4}$ in.
8.	Purchasing order punched	651–1–1	$8\frac{11}{16}$ in. × $12\frac{1}{16}$ in.
	Progressing card		(bought-out)

Figure 10.2 Purchasing procedures for a medium-size engineering company

3. They must ensure that information-entry is checked, particularly where the paperwork feeds into a computer system.
4. They should make suggestions to their management (perhaps to the O and M department) on practical improvements to form design, as far as their own departments are concerned.

If supervisors realize the importance of forms, they will be a more efficient part of the company communications organization.

10.3 Office machines

Mechanization. The introduction of office machines is closely linked with the concept of mechanization, which means the change from a manual method of doing work to a method which is predominantly performed by a mechanism or machine. Office mechanization simply means an attempt to simplify office work with the aim of tailoring it for machine processing. The simplification aspect should be stressed, since many people speak with unjustified awe of certain machinery, especially computers which are in fact merely slaves of the human mind. Admittedly, such equipment can perform mechanical operations and calculations at very high speeds, but its performance is always reliant on the input with which it is supplied.

Advantages. These can be listed as follows:
1. Office machines sometimes reduce labour costs, but it must be added that too few people take into account the (sometimes) higher cost of specialized labour, such as systems analysts, programmers and other personnel associated with computer work.
2. Machines undoubtedly save time and there is a lot of truth in the saying 'time is money'. Time-saving is probably the biggest factor in favour of office mechanization, whether we are considering time saved in the preparation of paperwork or information for management action.
3. If the accuracy of input to a machine is maintained, then the resulting work produced by the machine should contain less errors than if produced by a non-machine method. However, one factor can be relied on, and that is consistency. Clearly, a machine does not grow tired, nor does it daydream.
4. Machines allow complex analysis and processing work to take place in order to facilitate management decision-making, such as critical path analysis (CPA), design, and operational simulation techniques.

These are the four main advantages of using office machinery in the mechanization sense. It is necessary at this point to clarify our terminology, since there is clearly a difference between the following office 'machines':

a hand-operated stapler
an automatic stapler
a manual typewriter
an electric typewriter
an automatic (electric) typewriter (paper-tape operated)
a computer

Each of these could be described as a machine, but one normally regards mechanization as a step away from manual intervention, ultimately reaching the 'untouched-by-human-hand' stage when we talk of automation. Looking at our list, both the electric typewriter and the automatic typewriter are machines, but the writer does not see them in the same light as far as mechanization is concerned. However, it should not be forgotten that the automatic typewriter requires considerable human intervention, particularly if the work is not purely repetitive. The computer, at its print-out stage, could be described as a fully mechanized ultra-high-speed typing operation, controlled completely from the computer's memory store.

Disadvantages. There is little point in dwelling overlong on the disadvantages of office machines. They are now well established in a wide range of applications and modern business just could not possibly be conducted without them. However, it is as well to look at one or two points:

1. Some office machinery is expensive, requiring heavy capital outlay. In the field of systems machines there is also the problem of obsolescence. The O and M report will need to weigh these factors carefully in making a recommendation to purchase.
2. Trained operators are required and, in some cases, a high degree of training. Operators may be in short supply in a competitive market. A small number of operators can be performing such a vital function in their organization that a crippling bottleneck could ensue if, for example, they went on strike. Mechanized operations have this unique feature of a small unit of people handling a large volume of work.
3. There is the danger of under-utilization of expensive machinery.

These three points overshadow all other apparent disadvantages such as noise and special stationery costs, which can be overcome by good O and M thinking. However, none of the three are insoluble: for example, considering point 3, machinery installed for one purpose may also be used for another purpose or its time shared with another organization (as with computer time-sharing).

Types. It now remains to list some of the main areas of application for office machines, bearing in mind our definition of office mechanization: 'an attempt to simplify office work with the aim of tailoring it for machine processing: a change from a manual method of doing work to a method which is predominantly performed by a mechanism or machine'.

WRITING AND IMPRINTING   Examples include:
   Franking machines
   Addressing machines
   Typewriters (manual and electric)
   Automatic typewriters (tape-controlled)

COPYING AND REPRODUCING   Examples include:
   Photocopying machines (various processes)
   Spirit and stencil duplicating machines
   Offset lithographic printing machines
   Microfilming equipment

General aspects of O and M 153

COMMUNICATIONS Examples include:
  Standard telephone equipment
  Telephone answering (and recording) machines
  Telex and teleprinter machines
  Dictating (recording) machines (individual)
  Centralized dictating machine systems (remotely originated)
  Closed circuit television
CALCULATING Examples include:
  Calculating machines (non-print)
  Calculating machines (printing-type)
  Electronic accounting machines
  Desk computers (electronic, e.g. those used in design offices)
INSPECTING Examples include:
  Time-recording equipment
  Labelling machines
  Cash registers
  Weighing machines (including automatic)
  Timers (for example, telephone calls)
  Counting machines
PAPER HANDLING Examples include:
  Folding machines
  Paper shredders (for destroying confidential documents no longer required)
  Note sorting machines
  Parcelling machines
COMPUTERS In this area we may include data processing equipment which is based on punched card equipment, that is to say not making use of an electronic computer. Examples include:
  Computing machines (analog and digital)
  Card and tape punches
  Input devices (for example, readers)
  Output devices
  Card punching and verifying machines

10.4 Mechanical aids in communication

The flow of information through modern business organization is inevitably linked with advanced communications equipment. It is in the interest of the modern supervisor to acquaint himself with the various techniques available in his organization and on the market. It is possible that he may be able to influence his management to improve communications between his own and other departments. Some examples of communications equipment are discussed below.

High-speed written transmission
  1. Teleprinter systems

2. Telex systems
3. Telegrams
4. Facsimile—telegraphy
5. Document conveyors
6. Gravity chutes
7. Pneumatic tubes for document transmission

Teleprinters and telex equipment (1 and 2) provide the fastest transmission of written communication: both use machines fitted with special typewriter keyboards. The teleprinter system consists of machines in the same organization, linked by telegraph wire, while the telex system consists of machines anywhere in the UK or the world, linked through the GPO telex exchange. These systems have the advantage of speed and permanence of record, plus relative economy, compared with long-distance telephone calls.

Facsimile—telegraphy (4) offers the facility of transmitting drawings and actual copies of handwritten material by GPO telegraph equipment. Document conveyors, gravity chutes and pneumatic tube systems are all useful for in-plant operation when documents and specimens need to be transported at speed. It is obviously advantageous to design these equipments into new buildings, rather than install them later on.

Telephone systems
1. Internal telephone systems
2. External telephone systems
3. Intercom systems (for example, pocket-paging or bleepers)
4. Telephone answering machines
5. Radio-telephones
6. Audible staff-location systems

There are a number of different telephone systems available and the subject tends to be somewhat specialized. For example, modern centralized-dictation systems for typing services may be superimposed on to the normal telephone traffic, or a separately-wired system may be used. It is up to the O and M officer to evaluate the various advantages and disadvantages. The general factor deciding on which type of telephone system to use is usually one of economics through control. For example, we might consider whether to install a private automatic branch exchange (PABX) which allows users to dial their own outside calls. Factors to be evaluated would be the economization on switchboard staff, the speeding up of calls and also the risk of abuse due to the company's telephone system being used for private calls.

Intercom and staff-location systems (3 and 6) are very useful devices providing that they do not reduce the efficiency of the users due, for example, to objectionable noises. This explains the popularity of the very subdued pocket bleeper which requests the wearer to go to the nearest telephone. Radio-telephones are particularly useful in large site work where management personnel may wish to hold instant on-the-spot

General aspects of O and M 155

conversations. Telephone answering machines are widely used, particularly in sales organizations: the caller is asked to dictate his request and name and address. The obvious application is for out-of-hours calls and inquiries and also for small businesses.

Visible systems
1. Closed circuit television
2. Videotape
3. Document copying systems

Closed circuit television (1) has clear advantages in bringing groups of people together for meetings, over the screen. It is also a valuable instructional aid: for example, a large group of people cannot observe a machine operation at one time but the camera can make this possible for several groups of people not even located in the area where the activity is taking place. Videotape (2) has tremendous potential in business training, selling and general communications. A cassette can be inserted into a television device and a moving film is seen of the subject matter. There is a wide range of document copying machines available (3) and these are linked closely with systems work. For example, a copying machine will photograph a document and in a few seconds produce a printing plate. This can then be run on an offset lithographic printing machine to give hundreds of cheap (identical) copies. There is obviously no chance of an error creeping in.

Other systems
1. Normal dictating and transcription machines for typed work
2. Centralized dictating and recording equipment for typed work

There is a wide range of machines to choose from, using such recording media as discs (records), magnetic tape and film. Supervisors should remember, when dictating into such machines, that it is vital to speak clearly and to receive some instruction in the art of dictation. Centralized dictation consists of a large number of dictators speaking into microphones, with their voices being recorded at a bank of recording machines in a central secretarial services department (typing pool). There are many systems and, as mentioned earlier, an O and M officer may decide to recommend a separately-wired system or to superimpose the dictation-traffic on to the existing telephone system. Much will depend upon the normal loading of the telephone system. Advantages claimed are economies in secretarial staffing and speed of return and service to dictators. If an organization does not ensure that typists are given a reasonable proportion of other work, such as copy-typing, filing and general secretarial work, staff turnover may increase due to the continual use of headsets by typists.

10.5 Office systems

An ideal office system (or procedure) may be defined as 'a series of logical stages culminating in the efficient and effective completion of an office task. The system will be clearly defined in terms of elemental breakdown, equipment and manpower requirements, and the various forms used.'

Systems design. Efficient systems design is essential in the field of office procedures for a number of major reasons:
1. It will ensure that total operating costs are minimized.
2. It will ensure that the work of each department dovetails with the work of other departments.
3. Sound systems design helps to achieve a controlled situation, on the principle that it is only possible to control something that is understood and defined.
4. A written-up system can be a useful device for training new staff and introducing new management personnel. For example, they can be taken through the forms manual, thereby reaching an understanding of the various forms used and their importance.

Principles. The general principles of office systems follow the basic principles of work study in order to achieve least-waste methods of working. The major principles are as follows:
1. Each system must have been subjected to the work study critical examination procedure, questioning purpose (need), place, sequence, person and means. It is, after all, useless to design a beautiful system for performing a useless piece of work.
2. Least-waste methods of working should be sought.
3. Systems design should ensure that unnecessary duplication and checking of work is avoided.
4. Systems design should achieve the best use of capital equipment and the minimum usage and production of paperwork. (For example, run-off copies of master documents must only be sent to departments either needing the information, or needing to add vital information.)
5. Systems should be designed so as to have built-in flexibility-potential.

It will now be helpful to reconsider our previous example of a newly-introduced purchasing procedure for a medium-size engineering company which was discussed earlier in this chapter (see Figure 10.2). Figure 10.3 now shows part of the procedure in diagrammatic or chart form. Some interesting systems aspects are worth listing:
1. A spirit duplicating process is used to print internal-circulation copies of the purchase order, including a goods inwards (department) copy and a punched progress card for use in the purchasing department progress section.
2. On receipt of goods, a goods inward note (in duplicate) is written, in conjunction with information taken from the goods inward copy of the purchase order, relating to whether inspection is required or not.

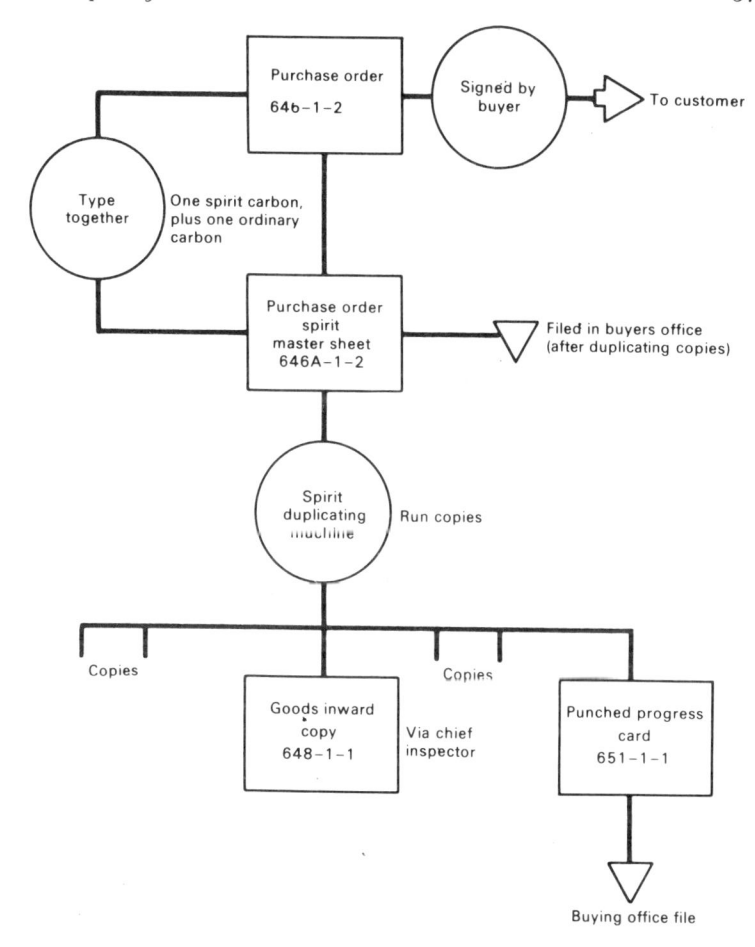

Figure 10.3 Chart showing part of the purchasing procedures (see Figure 10.2)

3. A copy of the goods inward note is passed to the purchase department progress section and receipt information is recorded on the punched card to assist with progressing activities.

Although we only have the space here to show a small part of the full chart (Figure 9.1, page 131), it can be seen that a system can rarely be designed with only one department in mind. Repercussions are felt throughout the organization and the need for sound systems design is obvious.

In the small part of the procedure shown at Figure 9.1 it is seen that several supervisors are already involved in vital office systems roles, namely the typing supervisor, the inspection supervisor, the goods inwards department supervisor and the purchase department progress supervisor. If these personnel are unaware of the importance of the office systems used, or are careless in their contribution to the implementation of them, inefficiency and possibly chaos could result.

Examination questions

1. Explain the importance of a major O and M or work study report and describe its construction. What steps would you take in order to ensure maximum possibility of acceptance?
(HND Business Studies *O and M*)
2. What is meant by the mechanization of office work? Explain in some detail the considerations necessary before management decide to mechanize an office procedure.
(HND Business Studies *O and M*)
3. Describe in some detail an office system in one of the following areas:
    (i) photocopying and duplicating
    (ii) a typing pool and machine dictation
    (iii) punched cards and analysis
   Describe the contribution of O and M in this field.
(HND Business Studies *O and M*)
4. What are the main factors to observe when compiling a report? Why is it necessary for a work study engineer to be skilled in report writing?
(IWSP Graduate *Method Study & Work Measurement*, 1968)
5. What are the four most important points to be borne in mind when designing a new form?
(NEBSS Certificate, 1968)
6. Describe the format and content of a work study report and define the main headings.
(IWSP *Method Study—Technical and Clerical*, 1972)
7. One section of a work study report should be allocated to the subject of benefits. What information should this section of the report contain?
(City & Guilds *Work Study*, 1974)
8. What are the main points which should be observed when making a report in writing?
(NEBSS Certificate, 1971)

11
Human aspects

11.1 The nature of O and M

Although O and M is based on a wide range of techniques, some of them of a complex nature, it should never be forgotten that organizations depend mainly upon people. Different groupings of people in organizations will have different viewpoints, depending primarily upon whether they are classed or class themselves as management or workers. However, there will obviously be other reasons for differing viewpoints: for example, professional people may look at problems or issues in a different way to non-professional people. The trades unions will certainly have their own viewpoint. Any efforts by the management to introduce change, whether by general management directive or by O and M or work study recommendation, should be linked with the joint consultative machinery.

O and M philosophy is probably best summed up and stated as follows: 'it is easier to move from the known to the predicted, than from the assumed to the hoped for'.

Objectives. From our earlier discussions on work study and financial aspects, we realize that objectives are needed in every area of a business where the performance directly affects the continuing profitability, increasing profitability or increased effectiveness. A business may be described as having six long-term objectives:

1. To improve the product(s) by giving thought (and action) to quality, uniformity, visual and functional design.
2. To improve the sales volume and services.
3. To improve profitability by seeking to
    (i) reduce operating costs
    (ii) increase operating efficiency
    (iii) achieve better utilization of personnel, equipment, materials and money.
4. To improve the company's image in the community.
5. To build better human relationships.

6. To improve the organization's ability to handle future conditions, such as changing markets.

Although personnel are only mentioned specifically in the above list on two occasions (3(iii) and 5), it would be difficult to separate the direct influence of good personnel policies and relationships from any of the six sections listed. After all, the whole of the organization's effort, as outlined above, is dependent upon people.

O and M and work study, then, are actively interested in all of the above areas. O and M will tend to concentrate on administrative areas and problems as far as its methods work is concerned, but where its organization work is concerned the whole company organization is embraced. In this case, a sound organizational structure will imply an efficient communications network at all levels of the business.

O and M has been linked here with long-term objectives because it must not be associated with any hasty and inadequate activities or recommendations. The true nature and objective of O and M is to be farseeing in its recommendations.

11.2 Resistance to change

That part of the definition of O and M which specifies the seeking of change is a fundamental one. In the previously-stated definition we learnt that O and M seeks to improve procedures, methods, systems, communications, controls and organization structure.

Although efficient line managers are always looking for better ways of carrying out their function, it must be remembered that their prime function is to attend to their main responsibilities. For example, a works manager's main job is to produce the required number of goods at the agreed quality to satisfy sales requirements. A purchasing manager must physically place the budgeted orders each week otherwise the whole factory would grind to a halt. On the other hand, O and M is uncommitted and exists without line authority or responsibility. The only justification for its existence lies in its ability to change the given situation, thereby improving it. If the writer appears to have laboured this point, it is only because it is a fundamental point, of great importance in the understanding of O and M.

Let us now examine a statement made by a famous exponent of work study, Russell Currie. 'Most people resist change, but management is dedicated to change, since it is necessary for growth and progress. Work study throws a great strain on the management structure, uncovering weakness; yet, for the same reason it can be a source of strength, spreading throughout the organization the spirit of restlessness and desire for improvement which are the marks of a dynamic business.' Reading through this quotation, step-by-step, the following questions could be raised:

Human aspects

1. Why do most people resist change?
2. Is all management dedicated to change?
3. What is the nature of the great strain thrown on the management structure?
4. Is a 'spirit of restlessness' wanted by most managements and is it, in fact, a good thing?

We can examine these extremely important aspects of O and M from three viewpoints: the individual, management and trades unions.

The individual. Change is resisted by the individual usually for basic psychological reasons, often linked with fear. It is normal for people to wish to have a stable life-pattern which includes both their working situation and their social life. Change can often represent a threat to this stability, replacing it with new challenges and threats of failure. A changing working environment can also create uncertainty regarding the future, fear of redundancy and the disappearance of old habits and associations, all of which might be regarded with suspicion.

Management. It is not always recognized that management too can resist change. Some of their reasons are listed below:

1. Managers may think that a desire for change in their departments, initiated by the managing director for example, is a criticism of their management ability and performance.
2. Efficient managements will, it is true, always pursue change, but other managements are content to settle for the present method of working, which is often the long-established method. In this way, some companies hope to avoid trade union activity and worker interest in the business. This can be a holding situation with low profit margins.
3. It is a fairly well-established myth that managers are efficient people and they often display tangible rewards to prove it: for example, management dining rooms (probably several different levels), company cars, well-appointed offices, the best coffee and cigars, etc. It is a good maxim that management should seek to uncover its own weaknesses and not wait for others to do so (outside consultants, competitors and auditors, for example). O and M is a management tool and management should be open-minded about its use. Unfortunately, exposing one's own weaknesses and failings may not be a desire of many managers, especially those displaying the tangible rewards just mentioned.
4. In many organizations managers are very busy people: in fact, they are quite often overworked. Change will inevitably bring strain on the management structure (and therefore on the managers), arising from such things as new paperwork, control and payment systems, and changed relationships with labour. All these changes involve much more work for management, initially, but the burden should eventually be eased by the new proposals.

Trades unions. It is a fallacy to say that O and M and work study are always unpopular with the trades unions. Mr. J. Crawford, a member of the General Council of the TUC, wrote the following statement in an article entitled 'The Trade Union Attitude to Research and Productive Efficiency' (*IPE*, July, 1954). 'Scientific and technical development is imperative to solve economic problems and to raise living standards, but not at the expense of the human factor. Technical efficiency will be more presentable and acceptable after being "humanized" in the course of joint trade union and management discussions. The trades unions tend to regard motion and method study favourably, and, together with increased mechanization and other industrial developments, see them as a source of a shorter working week, longer holidays and improved working conditions.'

In the early days of mechanization, there was resistance from workers due to a real fear of widespread redundancy. This has been proved unfounded and the three benefits listed above have been evidenced: the working week has reduced very substantially, holidays have increased several times over, and in many industries the working environment has improved enormously. O and M practitioners must take care that their proposals move in the general direction of these trades union objectives, not forgetting their earlier-stated objective of raised living standards through opportunities to earn more purchasing power.

11.3 Meeting ground

O and M and trades unions. We are dealing specifically here with points concerning the actual O and M investigations and implementation. Trades unions will require satisfaction on the following points:

1. There should be continuous consultation through all stages of an O and M investigation and particularly before any new scheme is introduced which affects trade union members. See Figure 2.3 (page 20) for an example of joint consultation before an O and M investigation commenced.
2. Management should make it's policy clear on the issue of possible redundancies as a result of method study application and new (or modified) incentive schemes. For example, are redundancies to be achieved by 'natural wastage' and retirements?
3. An agreed procedure, based on full consultation, should be drawn up for handling methods changes and the measurement of work.
4. Full consultation should be made on such aspects as dilution (de-skilling) of work, movement of personnel, radical changes in job specifications and radical environmental changes, should they occur.

O and M and supervisors. We are dealing specifically here with points concerning the actual O and M investigations, implementation and rationale. Supervisors will require satisfaction on the following points (including education and information where necessary):

1. The importance and economic necessity of reducing manufacturing costs through such means as increased productivity.
2. The advantages of a systematic approach to methods improvement rather than a vague or haphazard approach.
3. The advantages of actually measuring work, using the techniques of work measurement, rather than such dubious alternatives as custom and practice.
4. The advantage of paying more wages on the basis of more work done and establishing this as a sound meeting point with workers.
5. Supervisors should be absolutely clear on the basis of any new incentive payment schemes and should be able to calculate the workers' bonuses, if needs be, rather than automatically sending inquirers to the wages office.

11.4 Conflict

One of the outstanding workers in the field of industrial relations was an American, Mary Parker Follett (1868–1933), who was born in Boston (USA) and studied political science, economics, history, law and philosophy in a number of countries. In 1900 she began an outstanding career in public service, extending her influence to social centres in poor areas, and vocational guidance. She shifted her interest towards the field of industrial relations quite late in her life and began lecturing in business management when she was 56. A number of published works followed in the eight or nine years remaining of her life. She had a lasting interest in conflict and in the search to reconcile conflicting viewpoints and feelings.

Integration. In proposing integration as the alternative to conflict, Miss Follett meant to imply a combination of the best opinions from all sides, while at the same time not necessarily accepting any opinion completely. She adopted a practical viewpoint on human relationships and did not believe that conflict is either good or bad in itself but rather an expression of differing opinions and interests. She provided strong guidelines for resolving and avoiding conflict, rejecting domination and compromise, and promoting instead 'integration of desires'. The manager should aim to identify the best ideas and combine them together. Ideally, both sides should be content with a solution which is the best for the company because they are led to realize the logic of a situation through a complete understanding of all the relevant factors. In the face of such facts, conflict should disappear. This idea of the manager and subordinates taking direction from a situation is fundamental to the whole of her philosophy.

Situation management. The 'law of the situation' states that leaders should prepare the way for orders and new ideas to be received by creating the right attitude for acceptance, providing some stimulus for adoption and an opportunity for better methods to become habitual. An illustration of this situation style of management in a factory was the formation of *ad hoc* committees to assist the production engineering manager with purchasing decisions which involved large capital expenditure. A very expensive new furnace was needed and a new furnace committee was formed by co-opting specialists from different areas of the factory. Great enthusiasm was generated; the situation governed the work carried out, without individual kudos being sought.

Situation-type management is currently reported in Japanese companies, such as Mitsubishi, where workers hold meetings in their own time to discuss methods of improving quality. The system of control is centred on the workers, and supervisors are often included in these meetings, which are sometimes held at their houses.

Upward communication. Understanding and motivation can only be effectively communicated if upward communication takes place from subordinates, after they have first been helped to understand the developing situation by management. Effective communication achieves an increased amount of sensible and constructive co-operation and can change the strongly-held values and opinions of others without creating fear and confusion.

A manufacturing company employing around 1,000 personnel in light engineering arranged for the sales director to address a meeting of shop stewards on present and future sales aspects. The director was astonished at the interest shown. A number of the audience were obviously well read and could make reference to matters related to the marketing of company products.

The other person's problems. O and M officers and supervisors involved in O and M investigations and implementation can help avoid conflict if they make real efforts to win others over, which means trying to appreciate the other man's problems. In one company, shop floor personnel had no understanding of a manager's job. Individuals from the shop floor spent a day with particular managers in order to bridge the communications gap which existed. On another occasion, shop floor workers engaged on initial process work in a foundry were taken to the final product assembly lines at another factory in the group.

Action points. Those wishing to find better ways of managing situations may wish to take note of the following action points:
1. Bring real differences out into the open and face up to the issues, rejecting any desire to dominate people.
2. Reject compromise where it appears to offer an easy way out.
3. Think ahead and try to anticipate problems and opportunities, seeking to identify necessary group re-alignments.
4. Establish and maintain direct contact with your subordinates and attempt to eliminate fear in the organization.
5. Direct everyone's attention to problem situations, creating an

environment in which new ideas and methods can be expressed and discussed. If some direct stimulus can be given to encourage the acceptance of sound new ideas and methods, so much the better.

Although Mary Parker Follett died over 40 years ago, her writings will still be fresh in the year 2000. Man has made great technological progress since the industrial revolution, but there is still great need (and room) for discovery and achievement in the field of industrial relations and applied psychology.

Discuss the following teaching of Mary Parker Follett, relating it directly to your experience as a supervisor. 'Control is not a discreet (unconstrained) event but a continuous process. It is more than forecasting and prediction: it is creating the next situation. The aim, for example, is not to meet a strike situation, but to create a strikeless situation.'

11.5 Taylor's 'Scientific Management'

Frederick Winslow Taylor (1856–1915) developed much more than time study and the subdivision of work, known as elemental breakdown, although they would be a fitting epitaph in themselves. He also tried to establish basic principles which would apply to all fields of industrial activity. Many years later he explained his objectives as follows:

1. The development of a science for each element of a man's work thereby replacing the old rule-of-thumb methods.
2. The selection of the best worker for each particular task and then training, teaching and developing the workman, in place of the former practice of allowing the worker to select his own task and train himself as best he could.
3. The development of a spirit of hearty co-operation between management and men in the carrying on of the activities in accordance with the principles of the developed science.
4. The division of the work into almost equal shares between management and the workers, each department taking over the work for which it is best fitted, instead of the former conditions in which almost all of the work and the greater part of the responsibility were thrown on the men.

These principles, extended and applied, formed the basis of what has been called scientific management. It was unfortunate that many employers did not take advantage of the opportunity they created to build trust and co-operation between management and workers. Instead, one result was that work study gained a bad name amongst trade unionists in the UK. However, the seed of co-operation in the search for mutual benefit between management and workers was sown by Taylor.

11.6 Attitudes

An attitude is defined as 'settled behaviour or manner of acting, as representative of feeling or opinion'. Attitudes of mind are deliberately adopted or habitual ways of regarding an object of thought, and they are often at the root of conflict or opposition to O and M investigations and proposals. Two vital points should be noted:
1. It is the outward manifestation of an attitude of mind that is the important factor to consider in management.
2. An attitude is a reaction based on experience. It indicates not merely what a person thinks, but what he is likely to do in a given situation.

11.7 O and M negotiation

In this section we shall discuss the planning and negotiation of O and M assignments. The planning stage inevitably includes the selection of a suitable assignment.

Planning. The aim of an assignment should be to achieve one or more of the following objectives:
1. A direct (measurable) cost saving for the organization
2. Increased efficiency
3. Improved working conditions

Item 2 includes those projects which clearly improve the efficiency of a service to management, but which may be difficult to measure in terms of money saved. For example, increased efficiency may be very clearly evident in the reduction of time delays between procedures. Item 3 includes those projects which clearly improve the working environment in such a way as to create a more contented labour force. This may be done, for example, by introducing better workplace layouts, equipment and general facilities. Direct cost savings may then result, for example, from reduced labour turnover and increased productivity, but such benefits may be difficult to measure.

In the way of a reminder, O and M is deeply rooted in the same basic techniques of conventional work study, namely method study and work measurement. However, there are two additional aspects of study:
1. The study of organizational structure and communications as implicit in that structure.
2. A study-specialization in the administrative areas of an organization, in contrast to the shop-floor areas of manufacturing companies, for example.

Selection. There are a number of different sources of O and M assignments. Some of these are listed below:
1. A direct instruction from senior management, which may stem from a crisis situation.

Human aspects

2. A suggestion from a departmental manager that his department would benefit from an investigation.
3. A diagnostic study tour undertaken by the O and M officer, possibly including pilot studies.
4. A study of departmental and company operating statements by the financial director and the O and M officer.
5. A request from the shop floor, through the trades unions or suggestion scheme.

Supervisors undertaking study projects as part of academic courses (such as NEBSS, IWSP, IWM and City and Guilds) are advised to pay special attention to the selection of suitable assignments. It is absolutely vital for a student to ensure that the project is well within his capabilities, that it can be completed in the time available and that it will stand a good chance of achieving successful implementation. Supervisory students should also make every effort to attract management interest towards their projects. Some ways of achieving this objective are as follows:

1. Gain the direct interest and participation of your immediate superiors and other department heads in the case of a project outside your own department. For example, try to show the possible benefits to them personally.
2. Consult with the personnel department and trades unions concerned. This should be done at all stages of an assignment, including the initial ones.
3. Consult staff specialists, where available: for example, work study, O and M and financial officers.

Decision. The student should avoid making a selection himself, but it is perfectly in order to make three or four well-thought-out alternative suggestions to management. Figure 11.1 shows such a table of suggested alternative O and M assignments, drawn up by a two-man O and M team for management consideration, in a manufacturing company employing 400 people.

As an exercise (referring to Figure 11.1) imagine that you are the board of directors of the manufacturing company in question, which employs 400 people. The company is planning to grow steadily from its present sales turnover of £1.6 million to around £2.2 million in three years' time; there is no space to expand on the site, hence the high value placed on factory floor space (£6 per square foot); there is one hundred per cent trades union membership in both works and office areas, but there has been very little trouble in the past, thanks largely to a progressive personnel manager.

Discuss the five alternative projects outlined in Figure 11.1 and draw up:

1. An order of priorities for the O and M team, including any necessary safeguards.
2. An anticipated cash-flow statement, taking into account both commitment and actual expenditure of money on a realistic time-scale.

Negotiation. We have already mentioned in this chapter (and earlier, see

	Suggested project	Estimated O and M man-weeks required	Estimated cost of study - Time	Estimated cost of study - Equipment	Anticipated financial savings	Other benefits	Other remarks. Note: Assume cost of space: factory – £6 per sq. foot office – £4 per sq. foot
1	Centralized secretarial services	16	£1000	£2000	£5000 p.a. staff	Faster access to secretarial service	Centralized dictation equipment. Possible loss of skilled (short-hand) secretaries. 2000 sq. feet saved. Strong office trades union
2	Re-organization of purchasing department	8	£500	£750	£1000 p.a. plus unmeasurable savings	(a) Better quality purchasing (b) Physical proximity with materials control department	Physical move of purchasing department across factory to materials control department. 1000 sq. feet saved. Chief buyer will probably resist
3	Re-design of works order information flow system	10	£650	£300	unmeasurable savings	Considerable time savings and faster information flow	Closer liaison between sales/contracts and design offices and production. Present specifications system is cumbersome
4	Incentive scheme for the packing department	24	£1500	£500	£1800 p.a. staff plus relief of bottlenecks	(a) Early dispatch and invoicing (b) Space relieved for production expansion	Strong trades union. Any new pay differentials may cause trouble in factory. 3000 sq. feet of factory space saved
5	Computerization of wages and salary payment, production control and invoicing, etc.	92	£6000	£25 000	£6000 p.a. staff. £10 000 p.a. on stock level reduction	Much faster response rate in production control and commercial systems	Extensive systems analysis required. Large computer room required. 2000 sq. feet of office space lost

Figure 11.1 Suggested alternative O and M assignments (two-man team) for manufacturing company employing 400 people

Figure 2.3) that full consultation should take place before the O and M assignment commences. It may be easier to plan formal negotiations in government-type organizations than in some private companies. However, it is really up to the individual O and M practitioner to try to influence management to adopt progressive consultative procedures.

The O and M report should be a form of high-level communication in an organization and should provide positive feedback from the management team to the executive so that new, soundly-based decisions may be made. If the implications of the team's role could be grasped by all groups using O and M, there would be a great deal more successful O and M to put on record. The O and M practitioner should not be regarded as a lone-wolf but as a skilled co-ordinator or catalyst, needing the continued assistance of other members of the management team. The executive should spare no effort in order to achieve this.

If the organization of a company is a network of communications that should bind the organization together into an efficient working group, it follows that a report causing dissension and strife is not making an effective contribution at all. The following basic guidelines should be noted when considering the origination and presentation of O and M reports:

1. If possible, an O and M report on a department's activities should be submitted by the departmental manager, not the O and M practitioner. Ideally, the latter is a temporary assistant to the departmental manager.
2. Wherever possible, the recommendations in such a report should be agreed recommendations between the departmental manager and the O and M practitioner.
3. Where the report is suggesting changes in the organization and methods of a department that would also affect other departments, or the report is of a general nature (for example, communications), the approval of the respective line or functional manager should have already been obtained.
4. The accuracy of basic data from which the O and M report is derived is as much the responsibility of the manager or managers concerned as of the O and M practitioner. Full co-operation is necessary if essential accuracy is to be achieved.
5. There must be a foolproof negotiating procedure for O and M reports.
6. Wherever possible, managers should be encouraged to request O and M assistance rather than have it forced on them.
7. Where an O and M report includes financial implications, it should only be submitted to the executive after receiving the approval of the chief accountant or equivalent financial manager.
8. Claimed financial savings should never be overestimated.

9. Claimed financial savings should be clearly stated in relation to the recovery of revenue and capital expenditure and to possible obsolescence.
10. Wherever possible, estimated savings should be divided into two categories. Firstly, there are those which are as definite as a future plan can be: for example, improved quality control, raw materials or technology. Secondly, there are those savings depending very largely on the co-operation of the work force and trades unions. It may not be possible to negotiate some of these and at best a compromise may have to be accepted.
11. The O and M report should be presented in different forms to suit the needs and interests of its various recipients. The trades unions, for example, are mainly interested in proposed changes in wage rates, payment schemes, working conditions and possible redundancies, transfers or dilution of labour. The executive may only require a single-sheet summary report, listing the main proposal together with implications.

The graveyards of management are full of rejected and discarded O and M reports and there are many frustrated O and M practitioners. However, there is a way to achieve exciting implementation of sound O and M proposals and the above guidelines should help to guarantee this.

Implementation. Sound proposals are not only lost at the negotiation stage: many are wrecked both during and after implementation. Views on the responsibility for implementation of O and M proposals are varied and range from one extreme to the other. Implementation can be regarded as the sole responsibility of the line manager, once a proposal has been accepted by the executive, with O and M personnel taking no part, or it can be seen as the sole reponsibility of the O and M manager, probably working in conjunction with the equipment supplier (in the case of new machine-based systems) and also line personnel in the department concerned, as necessary.

Differing implementation procedures depend on a variety of factors, such as whether we are considering a civil service or government type organization, or an industrial organization. In the latter case, procedure may also depend on whether the executive really believes in O and M sufficiently to set up a strong department, give strong moral support to it and make a real effort to allay any suspicion and fears felt by line managers and trades unions. The following implementation responsibility and procedure is recommended in any situation.

1. The executive should never instruct implementation of an O and M proposal unless it receives the full agreement and support of the line manager concerned and also the financial manager. The O and M manager must persuade the line manager.
2. The O and M proposal should be presented by incorporation in a report from the line manager to the executive. (In effect, the O and

M department acts as a technical assistant to the line manager, helping him to do his job more efficiently.)

3. The actual implementation is the technical responsibility of the O and M department, working in its correct organizational, functional relationship with the line department. Nevertheless, a teamwork situation must be insisted upon between O and M practitioners and the affected line personnel. The leader of this team is the line manager.

Some of this will seem unacceptable to some readers. If so, the next point will be even more unpalatable.

4. Total responsibility for the implementation of the O and M proposals is with the line manager and not the O and M department.

Only by following this last point can the complete co-operation and involvement of the line personnel be achieved. It is a fact, anyway, that many of the best ideas put forward in O and M and consultancy reports come from line personnel. This is as it should be, with O and M acting as a catalyst. However, if all the persuasive efforts of the O and M and financial departments fail, and the executive are convinced of the soundness and importance of the proposal, the line manager should be replaced.

Mention must be made of the practice of parallel-running during the implementation stage. This involves maintaining a manual system alongside the mechanized system for a period, in case the new system does not work. This practice must imply one or more of the following alternatives:

1. The executive does not have confidence in O and M.
2. O and M have not explained and demonstrated their proposals efficiently.
3. The line manager is not co-operating fully.
4. O and M does not have confidence in itself.

The writer is in favour of extremely thorough groundwork before implementation, in an environment improved by the four points previously recommended for implementation responsibility and procedure. The new procedures should then be introduced as quickly as possible, and the old boats happily burnt.

Examination questions

1. What human relations problems would you expect to encounter in the introduction and application of method study to a factory department? What steps would you take to overcome or reduce these?

(IWSP Graduate *Method Study*, 1969)

2. Describe briefly four of the main purposes of joint consultation.
   (NEBSS Certificate, 1970)
3. Describe the main factors which you would consider in selecting a department for method study within an industrial organization. Once the selection has been made, what other factors should be established?
   (IWSP Graduate *Method Study*, 1969)
4. Write an essay on the human problems which may arise during a method study investigation, showing how you would attempt to deal with them.
   (IWSP Graduate *Method Study*, 1968)
5. Describe four ways of improving company internal communications and discuss their effectiveness.
   (IWSP *Industrial Relations*, 1974)
6. Explain why it could be important for a work study practitioner to have a knowledge of the factories acts and/or the offices, shops and railway premises act.
   (IWSP *Industrial Relations*, 1974—Selected)
7. How can the disruption of good industrial relations be avoided when introducing work study?
   (IWSP *Industrial Relations*, 1973)
8. Describe the psychological factors that would make an operator feel secure within the social group in which he worked.
   (IWSP *Industrial Relations*, 1973)
9. Apart from basic economic necessity, explain and comment on some of the motives which encourage people to work.
   (IWSP *Industrial Relations*, 1972)
10. (i) Describe the problems that redundancy creates for a company.
    (ii) Describe the methods by which the personal hardships associated with redundancy can be minimized.
    (IWSP *Industrial Relations*, 1972)
11. In a company which has not previously had work study, how should the first area for study be selected and what factors could influence the selection?
    (IWSP *Method Study—Technical and Clerical*, 1974)
12. (i) Describe the human problems that could be encountered in the initial application of method study to a group of workers.
    (ii) Describe briefly the action that should be taken to overcome these problems.
    (IWSP *Method Study—Technical and Clerical*, 1974)
13. Discuss the value of work study in relation to:
    (i) industrial safety
    (ii) quality of product
    (City & Guilds *Work Study*, 1973)
14. The need to minimize industrial accidents has led to the appointment

of more full-time safety officers. How can work study staff assist these officers to carry out their duties?

(City & Guilds *Work Study*, 1974)

15. Discuss how you would deal with problems arising from the introduction of changes in your department.

(NEBSS Certificate, 1971)

16. 'The test of a foreman is not how good he is at bossing, but how little bossing he has to do because of the training of his men and the organization of his work' (Mary P. Follett). Discuss this statement in relation to the practice of supervision.

(NEBSS Certificate, 1971)

17. What fundamentals should be observed when giving an oral instruction to a subordinate? Under what circumstances would a written instruction be preferable?

(NEBSS Certificate, 1971)

Index

Accountability, 25
Activity, analysis sheet, 74
    formulae, 76
    random numbers, 77
    sampling, 68 *et seq.*
Ad hoc relationships, 31
Allowance, relaxation, 52
Attitudes, 166
Authority, 25
Average, median, 61
    modal, 61
    simple arithmetic, 61
    weighted, 61

Breakdown, elemental, 90
Break-even chart, 5
Brech, E. F. L., 24
Budgetary control, 6
Business, long-term objectives, 159

Centralization, effective, 34
Change, resistance to, 160
Chart, alternative process, 104
    alternative routes, 104
    change of state, 103
    flow process, 100
    multi-manning, 105
    outline process, 99
    paperwork procedure, 113
    paperwork specimen, 115
    rectification and re-cycling, 105
    responsibility, 43
    summary table, 106
    time-scale (multiple activity), 112
    two-handed, 103
Charts, movement, flow diagram, 111
    string diagram, 108

    topographical, 110
    travel, 108
Coefficient, Pearsonian, 65
    Spearman, 67
Collateral relationships, 31
Colleague relationships, 29
Command, unity of, 33
Committee relationships, 29
Communications, equipment, 153
    mechanical aids, 153, 154
    systems, 120
    telephone systems, 154
Conflict, 163
Control, concept of, 1
    higher, 33
    purpose of, 1
    span of, 34
    statement, 124
Correspondence, principle of, 33
Critical path network, 137
Currie, Russell, 160

Decentralization, federal, 41
    functional, 41
Delegation, 26, 33
Discipline, 34
Distribution, skewed, 62
Duty, 25

Effectiveness, 4
Efficiency, 4
Examination, critical, 47–9

Fayol, Henri, 24
Follett, Mary Parker, 163
Form design, 147

Gilbreth, Frank B., 8

Incentives, definitions, 87, 88
Information flow, 131
Integration of desires, 163

Joint consultation, local govt., 20
Justice, 34

Labour turnover, 34
Local government, big business, 18

Management by exception, 92
Management services, concept, 10
    manager, 16
Manufacturing costs, division of, 7
Mechanization, 151
Method study, 8

Narrative, paperwork procedure, 113

O and M, aims, 4
    consultative role, 22
    negotiation, 166
    personnel, 9
    philosophy, 159
    report, 147
Operational research, 132

Paperwork problems, 119
Payment, methods of, 88–90
Performance, departmental, 92
    operator, 92
    overall, 92
    outworking of standards, 3
    rating, 51
PERT programme, 139
Planning, three stages of, 32
PMTS, 118
    established systems, 126
Power, 26
Production, batch, 40
    batch/flow, 40
    flow, 40
    process, 40
    unit, 38

Queueing problem, 134

Readings, number of, 63, 64
Relationships, *ad hoc*, 31
    collateral, 31
    colleague, 29
    functional, 26
    horizontal, 29
    line, 26
    line by-pass, 31
    staff, 29
Responsibility, 25
Rewards, fair, 34

Scalar principle, 33
Scientific management (Taylor), 165
Situation, law of the, 163
Specialization, principle of, 34
Standard costing, 6
Standard deviation, 60
Standard time, 50
Standards, reasons for using, 3
Statistics, descriptive, 59
    inductive, 59
Success, elements of, 2
    local government, 2
Systems analysis, 129
Systems, design, 130
    study, 130

Taylor, Frederick, 8
Trades unions, relationships, 18
    viewpoint, 162
Typing, 121 *et seq.*

Unity of objectives, 33
Urwick, Lyndall F., 24

Variances, labour, 94
    material, 95

Work specification, 85
Work study, definition, 8
    procedure, 45–7